Creation and Re-creation:

Experiments in Literary Form

in Early Modern Spain

Juan de la Cuesta
Hispanic Monographs

Series: *Homenajes* Nº 2

Creation and Re-creation:
Experiments in Literary Form
in Early Modern Spain

Studies in Honor of STEPHEN GILMAN

Edited by

RONALD E. SURTZ

and

NORA WEINERTH

Juan de la Cuesta
Newark, Delaware

The publication of this volume was made possible by the generous support of the following institutions: Barnard College, Colorado College, George Mason University, Northeastern University, Princeton University, and the University of Washington.

The decorated capital letters that begin each study are taken from the original type of Juan de la Cuesta's seventeenth-century Madrid print shop. These letters were graciously furnished by Professor Robert M. Flores of the University of British Columbia.

MANUFACTURED IN THE UNITED STATES OF AMERICA

ISBN (hardback): 0-936388-19-6
ISBN (paperback): 0-936388-16-1
Library of Congress Catalogue Card Number: 82-082504

We dedicate this volume to
our great friend and teacher
STEPHEN GILMAN.
It is his vision of Hispanic culture
that binds together
the generations of students represented here.
This volume is our expression of
gratitude for his courage, passion, and wisdom
which continue to inspire each of us.

Table of Contents

INTRODUCTION

IT MUST HAVE appeared to most Spaniards that the transcendent political events of the year 1492 had solved nearly all of Spain's problems. The fall of Granada completed the Reconquista, and the expulsion of the Jews seemed to guarantee the orthodoxy of Spanish Christianity. In literature, Spain appeared to be entering into what would later be known as the Golden Age. And, indeed, within the span of some twenty years, the Spanish presses issued a prodigious variety of seminal literary works. In the 1490's Diego de San Pedro and Juan de Flores published their influential sentimental romances. In 1499 Fernando de Rojas published his *Celestina*. Garci Rodríguez de Montalvo revised the medieval *Amadís* (1508) and appended to it his own chivalric romance, the *Esplandián* (1510). The late fifteenth and early sixteenth centuries also saw the first performances of the plays of Juan del Encina, Lucas Fernández, and Torres Naharro.

This explosion of literary activity strikes the modern reader as unprecedented in its originality. Yet not all of these works were original from a strictly generic perspective. Rather, their authors invested the received forms with new, often highly personal meaning. The results frequently signaled new departures, even for those genres with an important medieval tradition behind them. Thus, sixteenth-century Europe was for the most part to turn its back on the majority of the medieval chivalric romances and to consider Montalvo's *Amadís de Gaula* as the prototype of the genre. *Celestina* was generically a humanistic comedy, but its all-pervading influence in the sixteenth and seventeenth centuries reveals that it was read as much more than the last flowering of an already archaic form. We now know that it had become increasingly common in Castile in the late fifteenth century to stage plays as part of the ever more elaborate Corpus Christi festivities. And yet, it was the plays of Encina, Fernández, and Torres Naharro that gave rise to numerous imitations in the century that followed.

Despite important medieval antecedents, it was the sentimental romance as developed by San Pedro and Flores that defined the genre for the sixteenth century.

These works, and others, stimulated the imagination of their readers, and served in turn as models for the next generation of writers because, despite the familiarity of their forms, they voiced an awareness of new realities. Rojas infused the stylized humanistic comedy with a living dialogue that strained the limits of the genre by its very vitality. In his *Grimalte y Gradissa*, Flores complicated traditional romance patterns, fictionalizing the experience of literature, and thereby demonstrating a new awareness of the power of the written word. The re-presentation of sacred history became, for the early playwrights, an opportunity to address religious and social issues of the day. Encina's *Égloga de las grandes lluvias* appears to parenthesize the Nativity in order to express concerns unexpected in a Christmas play. Torres Naharro took the Roman comedy of Plautus and Terence and invested it with current anxieties, such as the anti-war sentiments expressed in *Soldadesca*. Gil Vicente often superimposed a contemporary preoccupation upon the court entertainment, as in the case of the plea for religious tolerance juxtaposed to the mythological plot of his *Auto da Lusitânia*. Virués expanded and ultimately destroyed classical tragic form, and, in so doing, paved the way for the Lopean *comedia*.

Each author made use of the old as a vehicle for the expression of the new. The works that resulted were striking in their immediacy and audacity. Their compelling quality did not result solely from the fact that they expressed contemporary and often urgent concerns, but also from the tension generated by the lack of complete consonance between the irrepressibly new content and the safer, traditional forms. In *Celestina*, for example, the received comic pattern of the humanistic comedy was subverted by the destructive treatment of the conventional ideals of love and chivalry. Rojas stripped medieval commonplaces of their comfortable familiarity by placing them in a context that gave them an unexpected and ironic meaning. The chivalric romance in the style of the *Amadís*, which celebrated traditional values of love and honor, acquired in the hands of Feliciano de Silva an element of self-parody that questioned the very values it celebrated.

The ambivalent treatment these writers gave to the traditional themes suggests that they did not entirely share the enthusiasms of their age. The period of restoration of order in Spain under the Catholic Sovereigns was a time of social ferment. The Spain of the fall of Granada and of the messianic predictions surrounding the reign of Ferdinand and Isabella was also the Spain of the Inquisition and of the expulsion and persecution of Spain's religious minorities. It is surely no accident that the seminal literary innovators were of predominantly *converso* origins or at least held in common modes of thought characteristic of authors known to be New Christians. More specifically, these writers belonged to the first generation of Spaniards to come of age under the ever-vigilant Inquisition. With the exception of Rodríguez de Montalvo and his typically Old Christian value system (a system that would be subverted in the chivalric romances of the *converso* Feliciano de Silva), that generation shared most acutely the *converso* dilemma of being simultaneously within and without Spanish society, of occupying an indispensable place at the very center of the social structure and at the same time being marginal to that structure. Mere spiritual alienation could not, of course, make for great literature, but where literary talent and ironic distance met, new modes of writing became possible. Just as daily living could never be the same after the establishment of the Inquisition, so the reigning literary genres had to be transformed, often drastically, in order for them to express the disillusion and disconformity of that remarkable generation of *conversos.*

In time, the writer's perception of Spain's changing social order motivated a corresponding search for new forms that expressed his consciousness of changing modes of existence. Alonso Núñez de Reinoso's *Historia de los amores de Clareo y Florisea* (1552) began as an adaptation of Achilles Tatius' *Clitophon and Leucippe.* Quite suddenly, however, the mere appropriation of another author's romance became insufficient to express Reinoso's own particular social situation. Leaving Achilles Tatius behind, Núñez de Reinoso used the pattern of the Byzantine romance to give voice to his own experience of exile and wandering. The *Lazarillo* has many important formal analogues, but none of them is sufficient to explain the bold creation of the picaresque form in the hands of its anonymous author. That he was profoundly disenchanted with the Spain of Charles V is certain. Equally certain is the fact that traditional modes of writing were unsuited to the expression of that disenchantment, and it became necessary to forge a new literary form to serve as the vehicle for the ironically exemplary life of Lazarillo de Tormes.

To be sure, not all literary experiments of early modern Spain resulted in forms that undermined traditional values. The romance of chivalry and later the *comedia* were for the most part conformist literary modes that reflected the ideals of love, honor, and chivalry that their public wanted to believe were the dominant values of their age. Affirmative literary modes coexisted in the Golden Age with modes that treated values more problematically. The prime example of literature that questioned received values was, of course, the *Quijote*. But Cervantes' novel was at least partially made possible by the existence of early sixteenth-century precedents that both affirmed and challenged the prevailing ideals of Spanish society.

RONALD E. SURTZ

NORA WEINERTH

Creation and Re-creation:
Experiments in Literary Form
in Early Modern Spain

Calisto and Orphic Music

Dorothy Sherman Severin

> El MAYOR REMEDIO que tiene es tomar una vihuela y tañe tantas canciones y tan lastimeras, que no creo que fueron otras las que compuso aquel emperador y gran músico Adriano, de la partida del ánima, por sufrir sin desmayo la ya vecina muerte. Que aunque yo sé poco de música, parece que hace aquella vihuela hablar. Pues, si acaso canta, de mejor gana se paran las aves a le oír, que no aquel antico, de quien se dice que movía los árboles y piedras con su canto. Siendo éste nacido no alabaran a Orfeo (*Celestina*, IV, 99).[1]

Celestina's words to Melibea about Calisto are based on Petrarch's *Epistolae Familiares*, 10 and 8:

> Quam deditum Musis Adrianum credimus, cujus intentio tan vehemens fuit ut ne vicina morte lentesceret? Prorsus mirum dictu: sub extremum vitae spatium de animae discessu versiculos edidit.... Nec fabulam Orphei vel Amphionis interseram, quorum ille belluas immanes, hic arbores ac saxa cantu permovisse perhibetur.[2]

I would like to suggest that the change of "Anfion" to "antico" is not merely a misprint as Miguel Marciales has suggested ("an-

---

[1] I quote my edition of *La Celestina* (Madrid: Alianza, 1969; introduction by Stephen Gilman).

[2] F. Castro Guisasola, *Observaciones sobre las fuentes literarias de "La Celestina,"* Revista de Filología Española, Anejo 5 (1924; rpt. Madrid: CSIC, 1973), p. 129.

tico" for "Anfieo"),[3] but is intentional on Rojas' part; he suppresses
the lesser-known Amphion to emphasize the more familiar Orpheus. This would not have been mere whimsy but is an example
of Rojas' turning traditional material to a new purpose. Here, one
suspects that he is making a humanistic in-joke for the benefit of
his original audience of university friends.

In 1489, several years before Rojas had added his fifteen acts to
the original first act of *Celestina*, Marsilio Ficino had published his
De triplice vita (Florence), the third book of which, *De vita coelitus*,
deals with the tempering through music of that influence of
Saturn and melancholy which is so common in scholars.[4] To
nourish his *spiritus* by absorbing part of the *quinta essentia*, or cosmic
spirit, Ficino sang Orphic hymns on his *lyra orphica*. The technique
was to imitate musically the character of the god after whom a
planet was named, in order to attract jovial, solarian, venereal, or
mercurial influences. It is likely that Ficino would have favored the
sun in the hymns played on his *lyra orphica*, probably a *lira de
bracchio*, which was adorned with the illustrations of Orpheus
charming the animals and rocks. According to D. P. Walker,
"Orpheus was a *priscus theologus....* In the series of ancient theo-
logians...Orpheus has a conspicuous place, because he is the most
ancient of the Greeks, the master of Pythagoras, and through him
of Plato. He is also, of course, the symbol of the powerful effect-
producing singer, and he was a magician" (p. 23). Walker goes on
to suggest that Ficino was the first Renaissance writer to treat the
effects of music seriously and practically, although he probably
tried to use this Orphic music for magical purposes to invoke some
sort of good planetary demons (pp. 48 ff.).

Of course the association of Orpheus and music was an auto-
matic one in the early Renaissance, and there is some evidence
that in Spain he was particularly associated with the *vihuela*, a large
guitar; an illustration of 1536 in Luis de Milán's *El Maestro*[5] shows

[3] *Carta al Profesor Stephen Gilman sobre problemas Rojanos y celestinescos a
propósito del libro "The Spain of Fernando de Rojas,"* 2nd ed. (Mérida, Venezuela:
Facultad de Humanidades, 1975), p. 75.

[4] D. P. Walker, *Spiritual and Demonic Magic from Ficino to Campanella,*
Studies of the Warburg Institute, 22 (London: Warburg, 1958), esp. pp.
3-24.

[5] *Libro de música de vihuela de mano intitulado El Maestro;* the picture is
reproduced in David Munrow, *Instruments of the Middle Ages and Renaissance*
(London: Oxford University Press, 1976), p. 84.

Orpheus playing the *vihuela*. But Rojas seems intentionally to have changed Calisto's musical instrument: in Act 1 he plays the *laúd* or lute, but subsequent references are all to the *vihuela*. Act 1 also makes explicit reference to the harmony of the spheres and to the fact that Calisto and his lute are out of tune: "¿Cómo templará el destemplado? ¿Cómo sentirá el armonía aquel que consigo está tan discorde, aquel en quien la voluntad a la razón no obedece?" (I, 48-49). However, when Sempronio is asked to sing a sad song, he turns it to a joke about Nero fiddling while Rome burned.

The jokes which Rojas makes at Calisto's expense subsequently are of rather a different sort; I believe that he is combining a sophisticated in-joke about the humanists' Orphic music, with the complex ironic contrast of the actual effects of Calisto's music on his soul. Calisto's music, far from transporting his soul to a higher plane or rapture, is, rather, associated with oblivion, sex, and ultimately death and Hell. Yet again Rojas turns a literary topic against itself in order to build a new literary form on the ashes of an old one.

To return to Ficino's theories, Venus is associated with music which is voluptuous with wantonness and softness; if this sort of music is sung often, the singer's spirit will take on this character.[6] Calisto seems aware that singing love songs will relieve the pain of love; when in the second act Sempronio suggests happy songs (jovial ones?) to divert the mind from thoughts of love, Calisto corrects him: "¿Cómo, simple? ¿No sabes que alivia la pena llorar la causa?" (II, 77).

The subsequent acts in which Calisto is shown singing, VIII and XIII, are heavy with ironies about death and oblivion. In Act VIII, Calisto sings a song attributed to Diego de Quiñones in the *Cancionero General*: "En gran peligro me veo; / En mi muerte no hay tardanza." Sempronio quotes Petrarch, and again Rojas links the obscure Sidonius Antipater with a more famous poet not mentioned in the Petrarchan text: "El gran Antipater Sidonio, el gran poeta Ovidio, los cuales de improviso se les venían las razones metrificadas a la boca. ¡Sí, sí, de ésos es! ¡Trovará el diablo! Está devaneando entre sueños." (VIII, 139).[7] Sempronio's sarcasm here

---

[6] Walker, pp. 12-24.

[7] "Antipater quidem Sidonius tam exercitati ingenii fuisse creditur, ut versus hexametros aliosque diuersorum generum ex improuiso copiose diceret," *Rerum memorandum* 2, 2, 20 (F. Castro Guisasola, p. 128).

is obvious, since Calisto plagiarizes another's work, far from composing by improvisation. The references to the devil and to oblivion also seem to be intentional, for after another original and fairly mediocre stanza, the fact that Calisto cannot tell whether it is day or night is emphasized:

CALISTO	¿Es muy noche? ¿Es hora de acostar?
PÁRMENO	¡Mas ya es, señor, tarde para levantar!
CALISTO	¿Qué dices, loco? ¿Toda la noche es pasada?
PÁRMENO	Y aun harta parte del día.
CALISTO	Di, Sempronio, ¿miente este desvariado, que me hace creer que es de día?
SEMPRONIO	Olvida, señor, un poco a Melibea y verás la claridad. Que con la mucha que en su gesto contemplas, no puedes ver de encandelado como perdiz con la calderuela. (VIII, 139-40)

Calisto is dazzled and blinded, like the partridge who is hunted by night with lanterns. The partridge, a notoriously sex-crazed bird,[8] according to bestiary lore, would also seem to be chosen intentionally to symbolize the sex-crazed Calisto whose music, far from charming wild beasts or leading his spirit to a higher sphere, seems simply to exacerbate his own condition of isolation and oblivion.

The connection between this and death will be made more clearly in Act XIII. After his night of love, Calisto's music has improved markedly; the stanza of "redondillas" with "quebrados" that he sings links strophically and musically with the end of Melibea's song in Act XIX:

Duerme y descansa, penado,
Desde agora,
Pues te ama tu señora
De tu grado.

But the sleep which he invokes is again a disordered one, and the oblivion will be brief, since Tristán is about to hear of the deaths of Sempronio and Pármeno:

TRISTÁN	Señor, no hay ningún mozo en casa.
CALISTO	Pues abre esas ventanas, verás qué hora es.
TRISTÁN	Señor, bien de día.

[8] See Alan Deyermond, "The Worm and the Partridge; reflections on the poetry of Florencia Pinar", *Mester*, 7 (1978), 3-8.

CALISTO   Pues tórnalas a cerrar y déjame dormir hasta
que sea hora de comer. (XIII, 185)

In Act XIX the singers seem briefly to achieve that desired
effect of Orphic music, but the singers are Lucrecia and Melibea.
Calisto receives the benefit of the music, but does not initiate it.
Lucrecia and Melibea sing to the stars:

Estrellas que relumbráis,
norte y lucero del día,
¿Por qué no le despertáis,
si duerme mi alegría? (XIX, 221)

Calisto seems to be awakened from his slumber at last and his
spirit is moved; he exclaims: "Vencido me tiene el dulzor de tu
suave canto; no puedo más sufrir tu penado esperar." When he
asks Melibea to go on singing, she answers: "¿Qué quieres que
cante, amor mío? ¿Cómo cantaré, que tu deseo era el que regía mi
son y hacía sonar mi canto? Pues conseguida tu venida, desapare-
cióse el deseo, destemplóse el tono de mi voz" (222). This foreshadows the twentieth act, when the music is replaced by "este
clamor de campanas, este alarido de gentes, este aullido de canes,
este grande estrépito de armas" (229), which will signal the public
mourning for the death of Calisto.

UNIVERSITY OF LIVERPOOL

Juan del Encina's
Égloga de las grandes lluvias:
The Historical Appropriation
of Dramatic Ritual

YVONNE YARBRO-BEJARANO

UAN DEL ENCINA'S eight dramatic eclogues, published in Salamanca in 1496, constitute the first important body of texts at our disposal in the study of the origins and development of drama in Castile. Although literary historians credit Encina with initiating Castilian theater, they also attempt to clarify the relationship between his work and previous dramatic traditions. Many critics assume that a medieval liturgical drama similar to that of England and France existed in Castile, but did not survive in written form. These critics suggest that Castilian drama went through a process of "secularization" in Encina's theater, which supposedly evolved out of this hypothetical tradition.[1] The investigations of Richard B. Donovan, Fernando Lázaro

[1] Leandro Fernández de Moratín, *Orígenes del teatro español,* in *Tesoro del teatro español desde su origen...hasta nuestros días,* I, ed. E. de Ochoa (París: Librería Europea de Baudry, 1838); Manuel Cañete, *Teatro completo de Juan del Encina* (Madrid: Sucesores de Rivadeneyra, 1893); Adolfo Bonilla y San Martín, *Las Bacantes, o del origen del teatro* (Madrid: Sucesores de Rivade-

7

Carreter and Humberto López-Morales seriously challenged the existence of such a medieval liturgical drama in Castile.[2] Critics have since begun to search out other kinds of native forms which may have influenced Encina. The studies of Charlotte Stern and Ronald E. Surtz, among others, have helped to mitigate the radical conclusion that no dramatic models were at hand to shape Encina's theater.[3]

Charlotte Stern has examined the relation of the early Castilian drama to medieval ritual, both sacred and profane.[4] Encina retains "many structural features and a theatrical perspective" associated with dramatic ritual: the interaction between thinly disguised actors and the spectators, and the overlapping of the time and space of the audience and those of the play.[5] Like Stern, Ronald E. Surtz searches for possible sources of these conventions which govern the handling of time and space in the early theater.[6] He suggests that the Mass and the court entertainments of the fifteenth century provided Encina with two models of dramatic allegory. According to Surtz, Encina's earliest dramatic eclogues

neyra, 1921); J.P.W. Crawford, *Spanish Drama before Lope de Vega* (Philadelphia: University of Pennsylvania Press, 1937); Bruce Wardropper, *Introducción al teatro religioso del Siglo de Oro* (Madrid: Revista de Occidente, 1953); Angel Valbuena, *Literatura dramática española* (Barcelona: Colección Labor, 1950).

   2 Richard B. Donovan, *The Liturgical Drama in Medieval Spain* (Toronto: Pontifical Institute of Medieval Studies, 1958); Fernando Lázaro Carreter, *Teatro medieval* (Valencia: Editorial Castalia, 1958); Humberto López-Morales, *Tradición y creación en los orígenes del teatro castellano* (Madrid: Ediciones Alcalá, 1968).

   3 Unlike these two critics, Antony van Beysterveldt in *La poesía amatoria del siglo XV y el teatro profano de Juan del Encina* (Madrid: Insula, 1972) believes that the immediate antecedents of Encina's theater are to be found in the lyric dialogues written by court poets during the fifteenth century.

   4 "Fray Íñigo de Mendoza and Medieval Dramatic Ritual," *Hispanic Review*, 33 (1965), 197-245; "Some New Thoughts on the Early Spanish Drama," *Bulletin of the Comediantes*, 18 (1966), 14-19; "Juan del Encina's Carnival Eclogues and the Spanish Drama of the Renaissance," *Renaissance Drama*, 8 (1965), 181-95; "The Early Spanish Drama: From Medieval Ritual to Renaissance Art," *Renaissance Drama*, 6 (1973), 177-201.

   5 "The Early Spanish Drama," 189-90.

   6 *The Birth of a Theater. Dramatic Convention in the Spanish Theater from Juan del Encina to Lope de Vega* (Princeton: Publicaciones del Departamento de Lenguas y Literaturas Romances de la Universidad de Princeton; Madrid: Editorial Castalia, 1979).

are analogous to the liturgy in their use of multiple roles (e.g. Encina-Juan-Salamancan shepherd-biblical shepherd-Evangelist) and in their temporal and spatial ambiguity. The Mass provides the model for the inclusion of the whole of historical time in the eternal present of the sacred event (pp. 64-65).

These inquiries have begun to illuminate the particular nature of Castilian theater, shedding light on the possible origins of the dramatic conventions in the early drama. But given the idiosyncratic character of Encina's early plays, we should be aware that stressing the formal continuity of certain conventions may overshadow the new function which these elements are forced to assume in a new context.

J. Richard Andrews' monograph on Encina is crucial to our understanding of the Salamancan's manipulation of these elements in his theater.[7] Although Andrews' work was attacked by R. O. Jones and more recently by Antony van Beysterveldt, it has been defended by critics of the stature of Noël Salomon and Stephen Gilman, and incorporated into the outlook of many critics of Encina and the early theater, such as Henry W. Sullivan.[8] Through painstaking textual analysis, Andrews arrives at the conclusion that the driving force behind Encina's artistic creation is his thirst for recognition and prestige. Psychological elements play an important role in Andrews' exposition of the "problem" which underlies the Salamancan's poetic production (for example, Encina's ambivalent alternation of commonplace poses of humility and arrogant self-praise). But we are most indebted to Andrews for calling our attention to the particular social circumstances in which Encina played out his personal drama. These circumstances embrace Encina's position in the hierarchy of late fifteenth-century Castilian society, most specifically, his conflictive relationship with his patrons, the Duke and Duchess of Alba.[9] Encina's desire for prestige, founded on his own assessment of self-worth, remained

---

[7] *Juan del Encina. Prometheus in Search of Prestige* (Berkeley: University of California Publications in Modern Philology, 1959).

[8] R. O. Jones, *Bulletin of Hispanic Studies*, 37 (1960), 249-51; Antony van Beysterveldt, *La poesía amatoria*, pp. 24, 26; Noël Salomon, *Bulletin Hispanique*, 62 (1960), 194-97; Stephen Gilman, *Romanic Review*, 51 (1960), 277-78; Henry W. Sullivan, *Juan del Encina* (Boston: Twayne, 1976).

[9] As early as 1921, Ricardo Espinosa Maeso commented on "lo mal correspondidos que fueron sus servicios por los duques," which together

unfulfilled in this precise situation. Many of his works reveal his frustration at the quality of recognition, both economic and artistic, accorded him by his patrons and other denizens of Castilian courtly society.

In the light of Encina's self-conscious manipulation of theater towards personal ends, we could ask ourselves how profitable it is to speak of the ritualistic or even magical function of these plays on the basis of their relationship to some seasonal activity, the contact between actors and spectators in them, or their spatial and temporal ambiguity. Stern states that Encina's Carnival eclogues (fifth and sixth) may be "classified as dramatic ritual,"[10] citing the points of contact between actors and audience and the fact that the two plays were performed on Shrove Tuesday: "it is this commemorative spirit that links the plays to dramatic ritual."[11]

with his failure to attain the cantorship "le indujeron a partir de Salamanca" ("Nuevos datos biográficos de Juan del Encina," *Boletín de la Real Academia Española*, 8 [1921], 650). Van Beysterveldt credits Eduardo Juliá Martínez for breaking with the traditional point of view concerning the origins of Castilian theater before the studies of Donovan *et al.* in his suggestion that the early theater evolved from the lyric dialogues of the fifteenth-century *Cancioneros* ("Literatura dramática peninsular en el siglo XV," in *Historia general de las literaturas hispánicas*, ed. Díaz-Plaja, II [Barcelona: Editorial Barna, 1951], pp. 239-49); he also anticipated Andrews in his perception of the self-serving nature of Encina's art: "Encina aprovechó su arte para sus fines particulares" (p. 250). He speaks of the "egocentrismo" of the *Égloga de las grandes lluvias* (p. 258) and points out how the Salamancan exploits the occasion of the theatrical event "para íngerir las cuestiones personales que interesaban al poeta" (p. 261). For Juliá Martínez, as later for Andrews, it is Encina's need for recognition which accounts for the very birth of Castilian secular drama: "el ansia de destacarse ante sus señores los Duques dio vida a un teatro que en aquellos días representaba una genialidad" (p. 262).

    [10] "The Early Spanish Drama," 190.

    [11] If dramatic ritual is not only commemorative, but primarily communal ("The Early Spanish Drama," 181), serving to draw people together, erasing lines between actors and spectators and expressing commonly held beliefs, the social satire in Encina's Carnival plays would seem to undermine a ritualistic function. On the most superficial level, Encina invites his courtly audience to mock the gross manners, uncouth speech, and ridiculous appearance of the shepherds who gorge themselves on their rustic fare in the sixth eclogue. But in more general terms, Encina seems to be satirizing the Christian community's un-Christian practice of gluttony just before Lent. In specific reference to courtly society, Stern remarks that for the noble spectators, the shepherds' *comilona* "could well

Basing their comments on Joseph E. Gillet,[12] both Stern and Surtz speak of the presence of confirmatory or anticipatory magic in many early plays.[13] Paraphrasing Bertolt Brecht, Eugenio Asensio has remarked, "si el teatro nació del culto, eso quiere decir que al apartarse de él se convirtió en teatro."[14]

The following analysis of Encina's ninth eclogue, the *Égloga de las grandes lluvias*, attempts to relate those elements associated with dramatic ritual to their new context: Encina's dramatization of his personal situation. The rains play a key role in his portrayal of conflictive social relationships. This analysis leads us to question the religious interpretation of the play as a harmonious whole in which the profane, historical dimension is engulfed by the "sacred time" of the mythical event, the Nativity. In the ninth eclogue, the Mass's paradoxical equilibrium of mythical and historical time is knocked off balance by the overwhelming weight of historical experience. It is a fragmented piece whose contradictions point to the concrete conditions in which it was produced.

The *Égloga de las grandes lluvias*, Juan del Encina's second Christmas play,[15] appeared for the first time when the *Cancionero* (1496)

be a parody of their own Saturnalian orgy" (90). This reading seems to be borne out by the text: "que assí hazen nuestros amos"; "nuestros amos ya han cenado/ bien chapado./ Y aun hasta traque restraque" (Juan del Encina, *Obras dramáticas, I, Cancionero de 1496,* ed. Rosalie Gimeno [Madrid: Ediciones Istmo, 1975], p. 168). On the most narrow level, Andrews suggests that Encina's social satire becomes more pointed and personal in the juxtaposition of the two plays themselves, implying a parallel between life in the service of the Duke and Lent (*Prometheus,* pp. 123-25). Rather than draw a community together, Encina's multileveled Carnival eclogues have the opposite effect of highlighting tensions and differences within society.

12 J. E. Gillet, *"Propalladia" and Other Works of Bartolomé de Torres Naharro,* IV, ed. Otis H. Green (Philadelphia: University of Pennsylvania Press, 1961), p. 496.

13 Stern, "The Early Spanish Drama," 181, 188, 191-92; in Surtz, see pp. 81-84, 104-11, for general discussion.

14 *Itinerario del entremés* (Madrid: Gredos, 1971), pp. 18-19. Although Asensio adds that we should not completely "ignorar o menospreciar los sentimientos y actitudes arcaicas soterrados en el teatro de eras civilizadas" (p. 19), he feels that Gillet was "descaminado" by theories which see a persistence of ritual in drama, not only of forms but of a "fuerza casi mágica" (p. 18).

15 The first eclogue, although performed "en la noche de la natividad de nuestro Salvador," treats secular matters exclusively. Encina's first

was reprinted in Salamanca in 1507, together with the play commonly known as the *Triunfo de Amor*. The date of the *Égloga de las grandes lluvias* is deduced from the text itself; the shepherd Juan (Encina) identifies the year of the great rains: "Pernotar, asmo se deve / tan grande tresquelimocho, / año de noventa y ocho / y entrar en noventa y nueve."[16] This play looks back towards, and crowns, the series of eclogues written in the service of Don Fadrique de Toledo, second Duke of Alba. The *Triunfo de Amor* looks forward to the plays of Encina's Roman phase and, like the second Christmas play, was written in Spain before Encina departed for Rome.[17]

The *Égloga de las grandes lluvias* consists of 256 lines which can be divided into four sections. During the first 88 lines, four shepherds describe the heavy rains and their disastrous effects on countryside and city alike. The next 46 deal with Juan / Encina's candidacy for the cantorship in the Cathedral of Salamanca and the following 58 with food and games. Encina dedicates only 64 to the appearance of the angel and the shepherds' desire to visit the infant and bring him gifts.

Critics have commented on the secular tone of the *Égloga de las grandes lluvias*, especially in comparison with Encina's first Christmas play. John Brotherton observes that the names of the shepherds (Juan, Miguellejo, Rodrigacho and Antón) "reflect a turning away from the biblical and symbolic in favour of the popular and humble."[18] Recalling the catechistic spirit of the second eclogue, López-Morales points out the new flexibility of dramatic treatment in the ninth; the shepherds' dialogue makes up the body of the play, the angel's announcement being reduced to a mere sixteen lines.[19] Sullivan acknowledges the play's "jocose, secular mood set

Christmas play, then, would be the "égloga segunda" of the *Cancionero* published in 1496.

16 Juan del Encina, *Teatro (Segunda producción dramática)*, edición y estudio de Rosalie Gimeno (Madrid: Editorial Alhambra, 1977), p. 119. All quotes from the ninth eclogue are from this edition. All quotes from the first eclogue will be from the same editor's *Obras dramáticas* of Juan del Encina, I, cited in note 11.

17 The *argumento* of the *Triunfo de Amor* tells us that the play was performed "ante el muy esclarecido y muy ilustre príncipe don Juan" (Juan del Encina, *Teatro*, p. 181), who died in 1497.

18 *Pastor-Bobo in the Spanish Theatre before Lope de Vega* (London: Tamesis, 1975), p. 5.

19 "Ya desde aquí, los pastores empezarán a hablar de sus cosas, jugarán, cantarán villancicos, y todo sin que el ángel haya venido a escena a anunciarles nada. Es éste uno de los momentos más significativos en el

against an intensely specific, local, and topical background," declaring that the "sacred Christmas character has been virtually lost" (p. 69). Stern sees the influence of the *Coplas de Mingo Revulgo* in the displacement of the conventional Nativity scene by "everyday concerns" and "graphic pictures of rural life."[20]

In his interpretation of Encina's work as "strategic answers to his personal problem," Andrews relates the secular nature of this supposed Christmas play to Encina's ambition and obsessive preoccupation with public recognition (p. 159). Here, as in the first pair of eclogues, Encina exploits a religious theme to "approach his own personal...problem before a public" (p. 126). As in other plays, the intention is fundamentally rhetorical: "to move the Duke and Duchess to recognize him and to act in his behalf" (p. 126). In previous plays, Encina centered his efforts on furthering his interests within his relationship with the Duke. Now, discouraged by the scant recognition he feels he has won from Don Fadrique, Encina attempts to marshal the Duke's support in the competition for the cantorship, a post which would increase his social and economic status. Focusing his attention on the second section of the ninth eclogue in which the cantorship is discussed, Andrews finds the same ambivalent attitudes characteristic of Encina's entire literary production. Encina's flattery of his patrons scarely conceals pointed criticism, as Andrews' analysis of the "votos"/ "botos" pun reveals;[21] on the other hand, Encina's pose of humility typically gives way to arrogant self-praise (pp. 127-28). Encina's

camino a la secularización temática del teatro castellano" (from the Introduction to his edition of Encina's plays, *Églogas completas de Juan del Enzina* [New York: Las Américas, 1968], p. 23).

[20] "The *Coplas de Mingo Revulgo* and the Early Spanish Drama," *Hispanic Review*, 44 (1976), 320.

[21] "The force of the pun 'votos...botos' reveals in epitome the ambiguous rhetoric which Encina is employing here. While pointing to the instability of the 'votos' (the possibility of influencing their outcome—with an incidental hint of anticlerical irony), it sets up a positive or negative classification for the Duke and Duchess according to their future intervention or nonintervention on his behalf. Actually, this has already been suggested with the 'si son sesudos.' As in other cases, the patrons chose to ignore the plea and failed to intercede to the advantage of their poet. In that action they were by this pun automatically branded as 'botos'" (p. 127). Andrews' explanation of the pun carries more weight than Sullivan's ("the issue...will be acclaimed shrilly ['agudos'], not in dull tones ['botos']," p. 71), although the latter adds yet another dimension to Encina's wordplay.

first pair of eclogues separated the secular and religious into two distinct plays; the ninth contains these two spheres within a single boundary. Andrews suggests that the *Égloga de las grandes lluvias* might belong to a "transitional stage...between single and dual representations,"[22] in which Encina "has telescoped what before was a two-part whole into a single play" (pp. 125-26). The structure of the ninth eclogue, however, is marked by the awkward shift from secular and personal material to the Nativity theme.

The play's popular nickname reflects the pervasive presence of the rains which have succeeded in usurping the place of the Nativity theme in the title. Encina postpones the representation of the sacred event in the eclogue to dwell on the impact of the rains. In his exploitation of this theme, rooted in the historical experience of his audience, Encina can count on a strong emotional response on the part of the spectators. But he does not introduce the rains because they are interesting in themselves. They help him create a space for the dramatic action of his play, which is carefully differentiated from the space occupied by the spectators. Far more importantly, the description of the destructive force of the rains becomes a metaphor for his own personal situation.

The role of the rains in the play represents an innovative use of nature in the early Castilian theater.[23] For the first time, nature provides the background for the dramatic action. The initial and longest section of the play presents the problem of the rains both on the level of description and on that of stage action. Although the characters do not immediately refer to the weather, their stage business would have made it clear that it was raining. In fact, the rain brings the characters together. Unlike many of Encina's earlier plays, in which the actors clearly inhabit the same space as the spectators, the shepherds' search for shelter distinguishes the theatrical world of the play from the room in which it was being

[22] Andrews points to the eighth eclogue "En recuesta de unos amores" as a structural precedent for the ninth, "containing within itself the two movements of prologic and poematic matter (the division here is actually made clear with a medial *villancico*)," pp. 129-30.

[23] Such an innovation may have influenced Lucas Fernández in his *Auto o farsa del nacimiento,* thought to be one of his later plays (1500-1502), where for the first time Fernández utilizes nature to set the action and create a kind of primitive suspense (*Farsas y églogas,* ed. John Lihani [New York: Las Américas, 1969]).

performed, and separates different parts of the performing area from each other. Juan and Miguellejo call Rodrigacho to join them, and he answers: "Aquí estoy, tras las barrancas" (p. 111). Juan's repetition underlines Rodrigacho's sheltered position: "Llugo, llugo te abarrancas / encovado allá atrás. / Ven, verás, / haremos dos mil quellotros." Juan and Miguellejo apparently cannot see Rodrigacho, since he refuses to reveal who is with him: "RODRIGACHO: Mas andad acá vosotros; / y, soncas, seremos más. / JUAN: ¿Y quién estallá contigo? / RODRIGACHO: No vo lo quiero dezir" (p. 112). When Juan and Miguellejo decide to join Rodrigacho, movement markers indicate the change in direction ("Mas andad acá," "Vení," p. 112; "Vamos allá," p. 113) as well as the greetings exchanged upon arrival. The attempt to delineate and subdivide the theatrical space of the play is insistent, though rudimentary. When Juan and Miguellejo join the other two shepherds, Rodrigacho refers yet again to the sheltered position which he supposedly occupied: "Ora, sus, sus assentar / tras aquestos barrancales" (p. 114).

The eclogue opens with a reference to the Nativity theme ("Miguellejo, ven acá, / por vida de Marinilla, / que esta noche ques vegilla / gran prazer acudirá," p. 109). But once the characters are all together, they begin to talk about the great rains: "JUAN: A gran abrigada estáys./ ANTÓN: ¡Para en tales temporales! / RODRIGACHO: Estos males / assí han de perpassar" (p. 113). When Antón comments gloomily on the shepherds' muddied clothing ("Todos estamos con llodo; / no ay ninguno bien librado," p. 115), Miguellejo tries to lighten the tone of the conversation, reminding his companions that it is Christmas Eve: "Noche es ésta de prazer. / ¡Callá, tomemos gasajo!" (p. 115). This attempt to create a festive mood in spite of the weather fails miserably. The physical experience of the rains looms far larger than the religious feast in the shepherds' minds. They seem unable to turn their attention to any other topic of conversation. The rains' hold on their imaginations is expressed by their apocalyptic and even scatological references to them: "RODRIGACHO: A mi ver, / correncia tienen los cielos. / MIGUELLEJO: Asmo, si no acuden yelos, / todo avrá de perecer" (p. 116).

Having established the immediate setting in which the characters find themselves, Encina now broadens the scope of the rains' effects to include the city: "RODRIGACHO: Di tú, que vienes de villa, / ¿ovo gran tormento allá? / JUAN: ¡Dos mil vezes más que acá! / Tanto que no sé dezilla, / de manzilla!" (p. 116). Juan describes the general destruction caused by the rains, passing from the state of the landscape to the human condition. This parallels the previous movement from the countryside to the city. The passage which evokes the flooded river and collapsed bridges ends with a reference to the "cien mil álimas perdidas" (pp. 117-18); to Antón and Miguellejo's questions ("¿Y ganados perecidos? / ¿Y aun los panes destruydos?"), Juan replies: "Las casas todas caydas / y las vidas / puestas en tribulación" (p. 118). The section comes to a close with Rodrigacho's violent curse: "Agua y nieve / y vientos bravos corrutos, / ¡reniego de tiempos putos!, / y a dos meses a que llueve" (p. 119).

The destructive experience of nature described in the ninth eclogue should not be surprising, appearing as it does at a time when such uncontrollable forces seemed to threaten social life more than they do today. What does appear unusual, especially in a supposedly religious play, is the negative cast given to the concept that the forces of nature are the work of a hidden will.[24] The rains are imputed to the supernatural in two separate passages. At one point Juan exclaims: "Ogaño Dios a destajo / tiene tomado el llover" (p. 115). Rodrigacho goes even further with the word "tresquilón," appropriate for a shepherd's vocabulary and also denoting loss: "¡Danos Dios gran tresquilón / ogaño con avenidas!" (p. 118). These comments have an accusative air about them, as if mortals were victims, reduced to the bestial level of shorn sheep in Rodrigacho's corrosive turn to the Good Shepherd image.[25] This treatment of the rains implies a vision of nature as an insoluble problem, over which human beings exercise no control.

The function of the rains becomes clearer in the second section. Encina now links the rains with his own personal difficulties: his candidacy for the post of cantor in the Cathedral of Salamanca, itself the direct result of his dissatisfaction with the Duke's patronage. Encina's creative use of nature goes beyond setting and motivating dramatic action or structuring space and time in the play. His true innovation lies in the transformation of natural

---

[24] For a discussion of such attitudes towards nature in earlier times, see Marc Bloch, *Feudal Society*, trans. L. A. Manyon (Chicago: University of Chicago Press, 1961), pp. 72 and 83.

[25] Juan's repetition strengthens the linguistic connection: "Pernotar, asmo, se deve / tan grande tresquelimocho" (p. 119). Rodrigacho's com-

forces into a metaphor for a state of mind or a personal situation. The lines dealing with the cantorship, which Sullivan sees as a digression (p. 69), actually form the real heart of the play, carefully set against the dismal background of the rains. The topic of the cantorship arises directly from the description of the destruction caused by the rains. In the process of moving from countryside to city, Juan is singled out as the one connected to the latter ("Di tú, que vienes de villa, / ¿ovo gran tormenta allá?" [p. 116]). After Juan recounts the widespread devastation he saw there, the key question comes up in the most natural fashion: "Dinos, dinos, dinos, Juan, / en tiempo de tal manzilla, / ¿para qué huste a la villa?" (p. 120). Juan's reply completes the metaphorical connection between the first two sections: "¡Año pese a San Jullán!, / por del pan, / que en la aldea no lo avía" (p. 120). On the literal level, the rains force Juan to go to the city in search of bread; on the figurative level, Encina refers to the Duke's negligence in complying with the patron's obligation. The Duke's failure to remunerate his services adequately forces him to seek other employment in the city (the cantorship). The descriptive passages of the first section include a reference to the "panes destruydos," the fields ravaged by the rains. This linguistic connection prepares the jump from literal "bread" in the first section to figurative "salary" in the second.

Driven to the city by his plight "en la aldea" (Alba de Tormes), Encina finds the situation there to be even worse ("¡Dos mil vezes más que acá!" [p. 116]), embroiling himself in the fierce competition for the cantorship. The post was eventually awarded to

ment may be of interest to those who study Encina's work in the light of his possible *converso* origins, together with Juan's reference to the Old Testament. The victims of the rains are equated with those who suffered in Egypt: "Con los andiluvios grandes/ ni quedan vados ni puentes;/ ya las gentes/ reclaman a boz en grito./ ¡Andan como los de Egito!" (p. 117). Francisco Ruiz Ramón interprets this and other passages in the light of "otras catástrofes no climatológicas," namely, the expulsion of the Jews in 1492 and the anguished existence of *conversos* in Castile, among them Juan del Encina (*Historia del teatro español*, I [Madrid: Alianza Editorial, 1967], pp. 31-33). See Ana María Rambaldo's *El Cancionero de Juan del Encina, dentro de su ámbito histórico y literario* (Santa Fe, Argentina: Castellvi, 1972) for the most thorough discussion of this question and Sullivan (pp. 44-47) for a summary of the evidence to date.

Encina's rivals after the ninth eclogue was written.[26] The "panes destruydos," which were among the calamities witnessed in the city itself, express Encina's fears that he will have no better luck with his superiors in the ecclesiastical hierarchy and, in effect, prefigure his failure. For Encina there is no "bread" in Spain. The cursed year of 1498 encompassed the great rains as well as Encina's dashed hopes and subsequent departure for Rome, where he prospered under papal protection. As he writes the ninth eclogue, he exploits the rains to load his specific misfortune with all the weight of the general tribulation brought about by the natural disaster.

The handling of the word "pan" in Encina's first eclogue clarifies the use of the rains and its effects ("panes destruydos") as a metaphor for social relationships. In contrast to the ninth, the first eclogue presents the flourishing production of bread. The Duke's land, the shepherd Juan relates, is so well cultivated ("labrado") that even the poorest wretch has bread. Later, Juan/Encina declares that his poetry is artfully cultivated ("labrada"), and at the end, the shepherd Mateo encourages him to stay in the service of the Duke. For although Juan has not yet received anything for his services (his poetry), Mateo assures him that he is not "a lumbre de pajas...ni te falte ya del pan" (p. 99). The first eclogue revealed that Encina already had reason to fear that the Duke would not honor his obligation in their contract of dependent relations: remuneration / "pan" in exchange for service / "poesía." But the bread imagery expressed Encina's hopes that the situation would improve. The contrast between the fertile, productive fields of the first play written in the service of the Duke and the wasteland described in the last eloquently captures the degree to which the situation had deteriorated. The Duke and, by extension, the representatives of the upper level of the social hierarchy bear the same destructive relationship to Encina's "bread" as the rains to the literal "panes destruydos." In both cases, we sense connotations of helplessness: people are victims of the rain in the same way that

---

[26] Surtz states that Encina had already lost the contest when the ninth eclogue was written (p. 97). Espinosa Maeso speaks of the committee which divided the post among Encina's competitors as being formed after the date of the play (650, n. 2). He comments on the hostile atmosphere surrounding Encina's pretensions to the post, who was "poco esperanzado...de conseguir la plaza, como se deduce fácilmente de los versos citados" (649). This is the chronology generally accepted; Sullivan assigns the date 1499 to the awarding of the post (p. 27).

Encina feels himself to be a victim of his society's relations of dependence. The theme of problematic social relationships extends beyond the boundaries of the second section of the play. A temporary strengthening of horizontal ties which then degenerate into friction and bickering accompanies the disintegration of vertical relationships. The inhospitable forces of nature cause the shepherds to come together for comfort and companionship. Rodrigacho holds out the promise of warmth and shelter to Juan and Miguellejo ("Vení, si queréys venir;/ ternéys lumbre y buen abrigo," [p. 112]). The playful withholding of Antón's name gives special importance to his presence, as indicated by Juan's pleasure and anticipation: "Digo, digo,/ ¡dome a Dios!, questallá Antón./ ¡O, del gran acertajón!/ Vamos allá, miafé, amigo" (pp. 112-13). The miserable weather draws people together in newfound unity: "Todos podemos caber/ a la lumbre rodeados" (p. 114).

These words recall Encina's earlier plays in which "there was a place for everybody," either in the palace (first and eighth) or in the Christian community (second, third and fourth). Against the backdrop of the unrelenting downpour, Encina has lowered his sights. His goal is no longer acceptance on a grand scale but rather a kind of peer solidarity, the chance for all to warm themselves around a fire. The notion of protection has undergone a similar humbling evolution. As we have seen, in the first eclogue the shepherd Juan exalts the Duke of Alba as feudal lord who extends military protection to those who serve him. Thoroughly disillusioned with the quality of the Duke's "protection" by the time he wrote the ninth eclogue, Encina replaces such intangibles with palpable, material shelter offered in the spirit of supportive fellowship by equals. The characters' insistent references to shelter and the special effort, unusual in the early theater, to create a protective space in which all four shepherds huddle together take on special meaning when we bear in mind the metaphorical parallel between the Duke and the rains.

Explicit references to the Duke and Duchess, accentuating the deterioration of the hierarchical relationship, enhance the feeling of group solidarity engendered by warmth and companionship. Miguellejo comments that Antón and Rodrigacho, in seeking cover from the rain, seem to have little thought of their flocks: "De ganados / poco cuydado se os pega" (p. 114). Antón openly admits his preference for the fire: "Más vale estar, Dios te prega, / al fuego carrapuchados" (p. 114). Rodrigacho slyly adds, "Cuydo que con

más cuydado / deven estar nuestros amos," an ambiguous reference which Juan immediately counters: "Pensarán ellos que estamos / pastoreando el ganado" (p. 115). This disregard for the obligation of the servant towards the master draws the shepherds
together vis-à-vis the figures of authority. It is as if the steady
downpour had undermined the vertical bonds which structure
society. In this context, Juan's response to Rodrigacho's remark
has social as well as natural repercussions: "¡Ay, cuytado, / quel
mundo se pierde todo!" (p. 115).

The fellowship created by the rains and bolstered by the ne-
glect of the flocks reaches the point of maximum solidarity in the
second section where the other shepherds loyally support Juan's
candidacy for the cantorship. Here also critical references to their
superiors cement their unity. Andrews has analyzed the "votos" /
"botos" pun, and Encina places another pun in Miguellejo's mouth
which refers explicitly to the debilitation of the protective relationship between the Salamancan and the Duke and Duchess. Rodrigacho declares that Encina is sure to succeed, "que buenos amos te
tienes" (p. 122). Miguellejo's retort gives a new twist to the old
proverb: "No están ya / sino en la color del paño" (p. 123). Rosalie
Gimeno provides the following explanation: "El refrán entero es
éste: En la color del paño estamos y no nos concertamos. Julio
Cejador y Frauca explica que se dice 'cuando la diferencia es tan
grande que no pueden venir a concierto' los interesados..." (p. 123,
n. 109-10). Besides bringing to bear the idea of "desconcierto,"
Encina suggests that his relationship to his patrons has been
reduced to "la color del paño," the livery which he wears as their
servant.

This solidarity among peers is ephemeral. The dissonance characteristic of vertical relationships in the play gradually permeates
the horizontal relationships as well. The tension which finally
springs the group apart in the third section was already apparent
in the first and second. This tension is directly related to Juan's
brooding preoccupation with his ill-starred candidacy for the cantorship. In the first section, when Antón urges Juan to tell them
about his experiences in the city ("Por tu salud, que lo cuentes"),
Juan snaps back: "Tú contar no me lo mandes" (p. 117). He displays
the same aggressive touchiness in the second section, when Miguellejo rather tactlessly repeats the accusations of Juan's critics:

"MIGUELLEJO: A la fe, / unos dirán que eres lloco; / los otros, que vales poco. JUAN: Lo que dizen bien lo sé" (p. 124).[27] The arrangement of the shepherds around the fire recalls the cozy atmosphere suitable for storytelling. But the story of the cantorship has turned out to be as depressing as the rain, and threatens to destroy the unity of the group. Rodrigacho turns from that unsuccessful avenue to the topic of food and games. He specifies the motivation for the switch as a means of keeping peace: "No curemos de estar más en más desputa. / Si traxiste alguna fruta, / danos della, jugaremos" (p. 125). Juan continues to link the food motif to the conflict surrounding the cantorship, referring to the figs and chestnuts as compensation for his frustration: "Por amansar estas sañas, / aquí trayo, miafé, amigos, / una gran sarta de higos / y tres brancas de castañas" (p. 125).[28] But the food itself becomes a source of dissonance when the shepherds divide it among themselves as "chips" for their gambling games. This strange analogy to the distribution of wealth happens to be unfair, even though it is carried out democratically:

RODRIGACHO Ora cuenta,
            reparte. ¿Cómo cabemos?
JUAN   Cuatro somos; no erremos.
            Diez, veynte, treynta, cuarenta.
RODRIGACHO ¿Cuántas sobran?
JUAN   Veynte son.
RODRIGACHO Repártelas otra vez.
JUAN   Cinco y cinco, que son diez,
            y diez para mí y Antón.
MIGUELLEJO Compañón,
            trócamesta, ques podrida.
JUAN   ¡No haré, juro a mi vida!,
            pues te cupo en tu quiñón. (pp. 126-27)

[27] Sullivan points out the "wry bitterness" of Juan's retort, suggesting that in this Juan displays characteristics which conform to what we know of Encina's own personality (p. 70).
[28] Andrews offers the following explanation of the "strong accent on eating" in Encina's Carnival plays: "a depth interpretation of Encina's concern with food and eating might...see it as a psycho-symbolic expression of his anxiety over prestige" (p. 125). Miguellejo identifies the acquisition of food as an essential trait of Juan/Encina's personality: "Essas mañas/ ya nunca las perderás./ Siempre trayes onde vas/ mil golosinas estrañas" (p. 126).

Juan himself, significantly enough, is the distributor, in a kind of wish-fulfillment of his desire to escape from the powerless end of social relationships. Having learned a bitter lesson about resigning oneself to one's "share," he is all too willing to impose the same conditions on others.

The games also split up the group into winners and losers. Miguellejo's losing streak continues and he curses his bad luck. Rodrigacho, who is winning, cannot resist the temptation to crow over his friend's unhappiness and his own good fortune: "¡Ora ganéte buen cacho! / Don muchacho, / poquito sabes de juegos; / no te aprovechan reniegos. / ¡Cata, yo soy hombre macho!" (pp. 130-31). To combat the misery of the constant rain, the group found unity in mutual protection and solidarity in their common place in the hierarchical structure of social relationships. This unity is undone by the very elements of those hierarchical relationships which plague Juan / Encina: competition and the unequal distribution of wealth.

At this point of maximum division among the shepherds, in the midst of lively dialogue and intense interaction, the angel's appearance announcing Christ's birth has the effect of an interruption: "Pastores, no ayáys temor, / que os anuncio gran placer. / Sabed que quiso nacer / esta noche el Salvador / redentor / en la ciudad de David. / Todos, todos le servid, / que es Cristo, nuestro señor" (pp. 131-32). The last 64 lines of the eclogue seem like a separate play, as the main concerns developed up to this moment vanish.

Some critics offer interpretations which consider the play as a consistent whole. According to Brotherton, the ninth eclogue belongs to that group of plays which present the ritualistic conversion of the *pastor-bobo*. In Brotherton's eyes, the play focuses on the "appearance of the Angel to the shepherds and their consequent conversion" (p. 8). To this end, the rains symbolize "the desperate plight of the World without the love and light of God" (p. 6). Brotherton places the section concerning the cantorship in a universalizing context as well, stating that it further develops the atmosphere of gloom and pessimism from which the shepherds eventually escape (p. 7): "They have emerged from the darkness into the light" (p. 8). Similarly, Bruce Wardropper interprets the disappearance of the secular problems of the shepherds in the final section as the "sublimation of their concerns under the New Law of Christ":

The emergence of Christian love at the Nativity had, in the *Égloga de las grandes lluvias,* transformed the *saña,* the discord, the bitterness of the cold, wet, disappointed shepherds into harmony and joy. In the religious plays of Encina the Christian event—Christ's birth or death, the consequences of God's extreme love for man—always produces this ennobling effect.[29]

There are various considerations which argue against such interpretations. The proportions of the play and the care taken to develop the relationship between the rains and the cantorship suggest that these sections constitute the thematic core of the play, in a particular and personal rather than a universal and religious sense. The idea that the shepherds are "converted" or "ennobled" by the announcement of Christ's birth overlooks the fact that not all the qualities they displayed before the appearance of the angel were negative. The process in which the shepherds move from unity to disharmony seems to have more to do with the theme of social relationships than with the religious theme. The change of tone in the last section appears to be less a restoration of harmony than an abrupt shift from one topic to another. Has the discord of the preceding sections been transformed into joy or merely dropped?

Brotherton feels that the shepherds are instantly transformed by the angel's words, and cites Rodrigacho's speech as an emphatic affirmation: "Compañeros, digo yo / que vamos hasta Belén / porque persepamos bien / quién es este que oy nació" (p. 132). Barely five lines later, Rodrigacho and Juan reveal that they have not grasped the meaning of the angel's message at all: "RODRIGACHO: ¿Quién dijo quera nacido? / JUAN: Cuydo quel saludador" (p. 133). Brotherton deals lightly with this complication: "Their sudden declaration of faith is only briefly interrupted by Juan's humorous confusion of the words 'Salvador' and 'saludador.' Apart from that, they are, to all intents and purposes, totally convinced and converted" (p. 8). Brotherton himself notes that the *saludador* "epitomises the world

<hr/>

[29] "Metamorphosis in the Theatre of Juan del Encina," *Studies in Philology,* 59 (1962), 45 and 49. Gimeno coincides with Wardropper in seeing the play as a unified whole whose meaning is fundamentally religious: the first three sections correspond to the world of the Old Testament, under the "Ley Antigua" (*discordia*); the angel's message transports us to the world of the New Testament, of the "Ley Nueva" (*concordia*). See the discussion of the play in her edition, pp. 3-12.

of superstition and ignorance that the *Pastor-Bobo* is about to abandon for that of the *Salvador*, Christ" (p. 8, n. 17).[30]

An expression of faith in the Savior on the part of the shepherds in thè concluding lines would strengthen this argument. But throughout the entire section they speak only of going to see the newborn child and of the presents they intend to give him. Encina emphasizes the humorous, rustic quality of their gifts, rather than Christ as Savior. In his first Christmas play, the second eclogue, Encina made an effort to develop the meaning of the religious event in positive, social terms. There, Juan / Encina, in his role as Juan / Evangelist, expressed the message of universal acceptance into the Christian community brought about by Christ's birth: "Todos, todos le servid" (p. 109). In the ninth eclogue, these words are given to the angel, and this time Juan / Encina, rather than affirming such a message, comically deflects it, perhaps insinuating that he no longer has faith in such a solution to his own and his society's problems.[31]

A major drawback to Brotherton's conversion theory, in which the rains symbolize the unredeemed world, is the persistence of the rains throughout the entire play. Just before the eclogue ends, Miguellejo urges his companions: "¡Vamos, vamos / antes que más llueva!" (p. 137). The angel's message brings at best a temporary respite from the rains.

Encina, although perhaps not an outstanding dramatist, was an excellent poet and a meticulous craftsman.[32] If the ninth eclogue's meaning lay in a coherent relationship between its secular and religious portions, we would expect to find that Encina had woven

[30] Sullivan cites a literary precedent for Juan's confusion in the *Vita Christi* by Iñigo de Mendoza, and sees both as developments of the biblical text, "...and they were sore afraid" (p. 70).

[31] Compare also Rodrigacho's lukewarm, somewhat prosaic reception of the angel's message ("Compañeros, digo yo / que vamos hasta Belén / porque persepamos bien / quién es este que oy nació," [p. 132]) with the same character's expressive reaction to Juan's description of the rains: "¡O, qué huerte maravilla!" (p. 117). Such linguistic evidence lends more weight to the natural wonder than to the sacred one.

[32] James A. Anderson, in his article "Juan del Encina: An Abuse of Form?" (*Romance Notes*, 10 [1968-1969], 353-58), shows the extent of Encina's scrupulous attention to form; the only two errors in versification Anderson could find in the entire *Cancionero* are purposefully constructed to make a subtle point.

a net of verbal cross-references and interlocking images across the two parts, as he did between the first and second eclogues.[33] An analysis of such structural levels of the play reveals that while the first three sections are tightly interwoven in this way, the fourth is connected only superficially to the rest of the eclogue.

A continuous transition from section to section marks the secular portion of the play: the rains in the first become a metaphor for the situation set forth in the second; to distract themselves from the problems related to the cantorship the shepherds turn to food and games in the third. This unbroken development is interrupted between the third section and the fourth: the religious theme appears to be, in effect, yet another distraction. The repetition of key words and images further connects the sections of the non-religious portion of the play to one another. This unifying device, more suited to poetry than to drama, is also characteristic of Encina's first pair of eclogues. Andrews has studied the image clusters of "bread," "light" and "shepherd" in the first eclogue and their relationship to the same images in the second (p. 119); earlier I discussed the repetition of the words "labrado" and "pan" in the first eclogue to draw a parallel between the Duke's bread-producing land and Encina's "bread-producing" poetry. Encina uses verbal repetition in the ninth eclogue as well to link the second and third with the preceding section. In response to Rodrigacho's question in the first section ("Di tú, que vienes de villa, / ¿ovo gran tormenta allá?"), Juan replied: "Tanto que no sé dezilla, / de manzilla!" (p. 116). The second section opens with the words "en tiempo de tal manzilla, / ¿para qué huste a la villa?" (p. 120), initiating the transfer of the emotional charge associated with the rains to Encina's own personal problem. Juan's first words in the third section ("por amansar estas sañas," [p. 125]), echo the description of his enemies in the second: "Muchos ay de mí sañudos" (p. 124). This verbal link is missing between the third and fourth sections.[34]

[33] See Andrews, pp. 110-19. In his discussion of the ninth eclogue, Andrews points out what he feels to be a link between the secular and religious portions of the play: Encina's projection of himself as wrongfully persecuted shepherd in the secular part is meant to associate him with the wrongfully persecuted Shepherd of the Nativity theme (p. 127).

[34] At times, the same word is used in different contexts to reinforce important thematic developments. One such example is the repetition of the word "pan" in a figurative sense to underscore the metaphorical

The only element present in all four sections is the rains. It is the major topic of the first and appears most succinctly in the second with the ambiguous "pan que en la aldea no lo avía." In the third Juan discloses the source of the figs and the chestnuts: "Topé con la gran tormenta / una puta vieja franca / que me dio veynte a la branca" (p. 126), a reference which continues to tie the food motif to the depriving rains / Duke. Finally, the play ends on the menacing note of the threatening rains. This persistent presence throughout establishes a cohesive internal pattern which points to the underlying meaning of the play. The references to "placer" at the beginning and end of the play set up an external framework for the obligatory religious theme.

The rupture between the two levels of the play could be the structural expression of its content. Those who see the play as a coherent whole may perhaps impose on it a harmonious vision which Encina was far from possessing at that time. His frame of mind may be contained in the play's very fragmentation. The problems which the play presents remain problems; Encina did not seem to find in the religious theme a workable solution.

More significantly, the fractured structure of the play is directly related to the ·material conditions in which it was produced. A familiar dilemma confronted Encina: the conflict between what he was commissioned to write and what he would have liked to write. Andrews has analyzed Encina's solution to this problem: he would compose a "prologue," in which he dealt with his own concerns, and treat the required theme in the "play." The development of this practice runs parallel to Encina's perception of the course of his relationship with his patrons. As the situation worsened, the "prologue," in which Encina subverts the theatrical act to make a rhetorical plea on his own behalf, took over the place of the "play" proper. Already in the fifth and sixth eclogues, the two parts are roughly equal; by the ninth, the proportions between prologue and play found in the first pair of eclogues are reversed. The ending of

relation between the rains and Encina's frustrated ambitions and feelings of helplessness. The word "caber" is made to trace the shepherds' movement from unity to division. In the first section it signals solidarity: "Todos podemos caber/ a la lumbre rodeados" (p. 114). It disappears in the second section, where the factors are introduced which break down this unity, and reappears in the third to draw lines among the shepherds according to their lot: "RODRIGACHO: ¿Cómo cabemos?" (p. 126); "JUAN: pues te cupo en tu quiñón (p. 127).

the *Égloga de las grandes lluvias,* which was to be after all a Nativity play, is tacked on mechanically to fulfill Encina's obligation. The product of such a situation is a defective play. Encina was trapped in a vicious circle. While he was in the service of the Duke he was obliged to write what was requested of him. In this, his situation differed little from that of other court dramatists, such as Gil Vicente. But Encina was peculiarly hamstrung by these conditions, largely because he tended to perceive his relationship with the Duke as a problem. In his eyes his service was never awarded the recognition it deserved. This gnawing dissatisfaction prevented him from dedicating himself wholeheartedly to the conventional theme; instead, he is led to the representation of his own frustration. The same conditions which dictated the content of his plays occupied his mind to the extent that the obligatory theme became the "pre-text" for a new content. It is significant that the break with the Duke marks the disappearance of these specific problems in Encina's theater.

Encina's Salamancan trajectory traces his growing awareness of the theater's potential for dealing directly with history, but at the expense of myth and ritual. Rather than absorb the historical concerns of the major portion of the play into its "timeless present," the mythical dimension of the ninth eclogue is invaded by the rains which function as a metaphor for Encina's personal experience. Ironically, the commission to write "ritual" plays provided Encina with the "bread" he needed, but did not affirm the miraculous power of ritual to interrupt history. The problems not adequately solved in the ninth and preceding eclogues are worked out "off-stage" with Encina's move to Rome and subsequent social and economic ascent.

UNIVERSITY OF WASHINGTON

Torres Naharro's
Anti-War Play

NORA WEINERTH

OMEDIA SOLDADESCA is about an attempt at recruiting a five-hundred man papal army. Few soliders can be persuaded to join, and those who enlist do so half-heartedly, and only for the money. The whole enterprise is presented as trivial and finally absurd: the very captain who recruits the men in the beginning steals their salaries in the end, and that marks the end of both the papal army and the play.

The play was probably inspired by the lengthy papal wars in Italy, in which Torres Naharro may have participated. We know that his patron, Bernardino de Carvajal, Cardinal of Santa Cruz, had hoped to be elected pope in 1503. When the cardinal's ambition was thwarted, he waged a war against Pope Julius II that lasted until Julius' death in 1513. The succeeding pope, Leo X, effected a reconciliation between the excommunicated cardinal and the papacy, and the ten-year conflict came to an end.[1]

Soldadesca might have been written to celebrate the end of the rift between Torres Naharro's patron and the Church.[2] But the

---

[1] For a brief account of the rift between Carvajal and Julius II, see Marcelino Menéndez Pelayo, *Bartolomé de Torres Naharro y su "Propaladia."* *Estudio preliminar* (Madrid: F. Fé, 1900), pp. 8-9.

[2] If so, the play must have been performed some time after Leo's election in 1513. We know that Soldadesca enjoyed immediate success. It

play is more than a vindication of the dramatist's patron, and it does more than discredit the cardinal's bitter enemy, the ruthlessly ambitious and warlike Julius II.[3] As he did in other plays, in *Soldadesca* Torres Naharro went far beyond the immediate circumstances that called for the performance of a play. In *Soldadesca* he articulated a highly personal statement on the chaotic age in which he lived.

While the political alliance between Carvajal and the new pope might have called for unambiguous celebration, *Soldadesca* was rife with ambiguity. The play might have been expected to confirm the historical significance of the reconciliation, but rather than glorify the event, the performance seemed to trivialize it. Not only did *Soldadesca* undermine its own celebratory purpose, but in so doing, it challenged the significance of the very history it was meant to exalt. Torres Naharro's play unfolded to reveal a series of gestures, none of which is consonant with the celebration of a great event. *Soldadesca* belied the grand gesture that perhaps falsely perceived great events call for, and it expressed a deeply-felt conviction that the grand gesture in fact bears little resemblance to the series of small, often comic, more often anguished, and finally ephemeral gestures that make up the history of ordinary men. What *Soldadesca* celebrated was precisely the series of small gestures, born of the deepest, most urgent human needs.

Traditional criticism has fallen short in its understanding of *Soldadesca*. Moratín proposed that the play "no tiene particular interés, ni se busque en ella objeto moral."[4] Menéndez Pelayo

appears that the cardinal and perhaps even the pope were in the audience, and Menéndez Pelayo believed that either Carvajal or Leo X himself asked that a *suelta* of the play be printed. The following entry in Fernando Colón's Registrum suggests that a *suelta*, now lost, was circulated before the publication of *Propalladia* in 1517: "Bartolomé de Torres; comedia Soldadesca en español" (Menéndez Pelayo, *Bartolomé de Torres Naharro*, pp. 37-38). For dating *Soldadesca*, see Joseph E. Gillet, *"Propalladia" and Other Works of Bartolomé de Torres Naharro*, 4 vols. (Bryn Mawr and Philadelphia, 1943-61), vol. III, p. 406 and vol. IV, p. 503. All quotations from *Soldadesca* are taken from Gillet's edition, vol. II. Act and line numbers are indicated in parentheses.

[3] For the case against Julius II in the play, see Stanislav Zimic, "El pensamiento satírico y humanístico de Torres Naharro," *Boletín de la Biblioteca Menéndez Pelayo*, 53 (1977), 110-17.

[4] Leandro Fernández de Moratín, *Obras completas*, vol. I: *Orígenes del teatro español* (Madrid: Real Academia de la Historia, 1830), p. 136.

admired it as a *costumbrista* portrait of martial *mores* meant to "arrancar fáciles carcajadas a León X," but he warned that "no hay que pedir más de lo que el autor quiso poner en ello."[5] María Rosa Lida de Malkiel focused on the "insincerity" of such judgements, and suggested their harshness was perhaps a product of the Neoclassical mind, with its distaste for rambling works such as *Soldadesca* and *Numancia*.[6] Gillet also understood the play better than his nineteenth-century predecessors: "It is probably a mistake to assume that Torres Naharro had no 'objeto moral.' The play is an exposure of rascality."[7] In this vein, a recent study by Stanislav Zimic considers *Soldadesca* as an exposé of the Spanish mercenary on Italian soil.[8] What has yet to be shown is that *Soldadesca* presents a superbly controlled vision of a crumbling world.

The play begins with the *Introyto*, in which a Spanish rustic, probably played by Torres Naharro himself, appears before his glittering audience of Italians and exiled Spaniards to announce an entertainment. In direct contrast to the festive atmosphere of the banquet preceding the performance, the mood of the rustic is clearly contentious. He commands attention with an abrupt "¿Qué hazéys?" (Introyto, 5), and then answers his question, equivocally, by airing his grievances against his betters in the audience. The traditional *pullas* are now transformed into a series of *preguntas* and *respuestas* that are, at best, inappropriate to the occasion and, at worst, openly polemical in intent: "¿Quién duerme más satisfecho, / yo de noche en un pajar, / o el Papa en su rico lecho?" (Introyto, 57-59); "... dais al Papa vn faysán / y no come d'él dos granos; / yo tras los ajos y el pan / me quiero engollir las manos" (Introyto, 66-69).

There is more in this outburst than the topical praise of country life. The audience no doubt laughed at the rustic's proclamations of the superiority of his *pajar* over their *rico lecho*, his *ajos* over their *faysán*, and his own worth over theirs. But there is also an undercurrent of subversion in the rustic's tirade, an ominous attitude that must not have escaped the exiled Spaniards at the

5 Menéndez Pelayo, *Bartolomé de Torres Naharro*, pp. 105-06.

6 María Rosa Lida de Malkiel, *La originalidad artística de "La Celestina"* (Buenos Aires: EUDEBA, 1962), p. 62.

7 Gillet, vol. IV, p. 509.

8 Zimic, "El pensamiento satírico y humanístico de Torres Naharro," pp. 61-117.

banquet. The rustic's speech, on the surface a comic condemnation of a decadent pope who recalls Leo's predecessor, also plays on the complex relationship between *villano* and the Spaniards in the audience, who brought with them a peculiarly Spanish contempt for the *villano* and his values. When the rustic identifies himself as a *villano* and a Christian ("Yo, villano... biuo como christiano / por aquestas manos mías. / Vos, señores... coméis de los sudores / de pobres manos ajenas" [Introyto, 75-84]), he is indicting more than the less-than-Christian ways of a corrupt pope and an indolent nobility. His attack is aimed also at those in the audience who were *conversos*, whose claims to Christianity may have been recent and a source of great social tensions both in Spain and among Spaniards in exile. The mood set by the rustic is unmistakably divisive, and it sets the stage for the divisiveness that characterizes *Soldadesca* from beginning to end. To the extent that it evokes a complex network of problematic social relationships, the *Introyto* announces more than an evening's entertainment; it foreshadows the end of an age.

The play itself opens on an Italian street on a hot summer day. The Spanish soldier Guzmán enters, cursing. He has been roaming the streets, beside himself with hunger and rage: "Para buscar de comer / quien no tiene otra codicia, / cierto no era menester / en Roma tanta justicia" (I, 11-14). Worse than hunger, there is no one in Rome "quien mire a la persona" (I, 17). Now his soliloquy captures the spiritual landscape of the play: "No sabéis adónde os yr, / todo el mundo está perdido..." (I, 21-22). Loss of manhood, a feeling of anonymity, disorientation, and a nagging hunger are the rewards of the victorious Spanish soldier. As Guzmán describes his predicament, we become aware of being in a land devastated by war. His lament registers violent shifts in mood, ranging from fury to despondent self-mockery. He considers becoming a mendicant friar, or a petty thief, revealing in the process a fragment of his past as a galley-slave: "Pues ya sé bien remar / y hazer sogas y lazos, / no puedo sino ganar / vnos pocos anguilazos" (I, 87-90). The blurring of identities between criminal and beggar is ominous and ironic. Such are the options available to the Spanish solider who, when the wars are over, has lost his *raison d'être*, to say nothing of his sustenance: "todo el mundo está callado, / sobra la paz por la tierra / sino a mí, pobre soldado / que la paz me hace guerra" (I, 36-40). Guzmán's options, as he sees them, reveal the extent to which his world has turned topsy-turvy. He reminisces on better times, when he accompanied Cesare Borgia on his nightly rounds, but soon nostalgia gives way to bitter self-parody as he longs for the days he spent in the galleys. When the Spanish Captain enters, he notices that Guzmán "deve andar muerto de sed" (I, 96). The Captain brings good news: a five-hundred man army has to be raised for the pope. Guzmán presents his military credentials, and the Captain replies, "ya sé que por vuestra mano / cresce la fama española" (I, 152). This is a sarcastic retort, because we soon learn what the Captain really thinks of Guzmán. There is a double irony here, if we consider that this is Torres Naharro's view of Spanish fame, with soldiers such as Guzmán as agents of that renown. But the ironies continue: "¿Vístesme en Garellano?," Guzmán asks. "Y aun os ui en Chirinola," responds the Captain (I, 153-54). Guzmán's reference to his participation in the battle of Garigliano is less a boast than an attempt to root his identity in the concrete experience of military momentousness. The irony is that while Guzmán means to validate his worth as a soldier, the Captain and the audience know that the battles of Garigliano and Cerignola were Pyrrhic victories in which the Spanish suffered enormous human losses.[9]

When Guzmán leaves to muster more men, the Captain turns to his servant and asks, "¿tú conosces a Guzmán / que haze de cauallero?" (I, 181-82). The servant knows him: "su padre fue vn açacán, / y él ha sido vn melcochero" (I, 183-84). We soon learn that speculations about identity are inseparable from questions about *linaje*. We know that mockery of the lineage of the Guzmanes was to become commonplace in the literature of the times.[10] It was the *conversos* who brought to Italy a false sense of *hidalguía*.[11] Guzmán is of humble origins, we learn, and the Spaniards in the audience might have recognized in him a familiar kind of *converso*. The son of a hawker of sweetmeats, and himself once a peddler of molasses, Guzmán in the Captain's eyes is full of "presunción" and "fantasía" (I, 186 ff.). The *presunción* of the *converso*, particularly when passing

9 Gillet, vol. III, pp. 403-06.

10 Américo Castro, *España en su historia* (Buenos Aires: Losada, 1948), pp. 663-67, and Gillet, vol. III, p. 408.

11 Stephen Gilman, *The Spain of Fernando de Rojas* (Princeton: Princeton University Press, 1972), pp. 141 ff. Also Castro, *La realidad histórica de España*, tercera edición renovada (México: Porrúa, 1966), pp. 266 ff.

himself off as a member of the Old Christian nobility, was a source of great irritation to both Italians and fellow Spaniards. With this as background, it is easy to understand the Captain's excessive rage against Guzmán, for now Guzmán represents a whole type to whom the Captain "les quiere quebrar los ojos" (I, 204). The violent reactions that Guzmán inspires in the Captain and his servant effectively evoke the social tensions that characterized Spanish existence.

But Guzmán is not the only type of soldier we meet in *Soldadesca*. Torres Naharro's portrayal of the *bisoños*, or new recruits, is among the most compassionate in the entire play. Upon entering, the *bisoño* Juan curses himself for having left his family and home: "...mal año y negra vejez / meresce el puto jodido / que se tenía en Xerez / vn real y mantenido" (II, 86-89). Displaced, like everyone else in *Soldadesca*, Juan tries to preserve his bonds, no matter how tenuous, with his former life. He, like the rest, is willing to join the papal army, not because he believes in it, but for the same reason he joined the Spanish forces in Italy: "Y por ellos [mis hijitos], / como quien por los cabellos / soy salido de mi tierra, / y a buscar de mantenellos / en esta maldita guerra" (II, 105-09). His friend, the *bisoño* Pero Pardo, reveals his own bitterness and disillusionment with soldiering: "poner la vida en el tabrero / bouería es de soldados; / yo digo que más quiero / la vida que tres ducados" (II, 131-34). And yet, soldiering did make sense in the not so distant past to these men. A moment of self-revelation occurs when Juan expresses his distaste for muskets in an outburst that would befit Don Quijote: "No me agrada; que en la guerra de Granada, / bien se acuerda Pero Pardo / que allá no estimavan nada / sino buena lança y dardo" (II, 146-49). So the *bisoños*, it turns out, are veterans of the war of Granada. But, confronted with modern warfare, Pero and Juan—witnesses to better days—are now bewildered and angry, understandably dislocated from new times.

A sense of honor is conspicuously absent from the play. Not even in passing are the wars referred to as glorious, nor even as necessary. There is, just once, an attempt on the Captain's part to speak in lofty terms as he encourages the men to join the papal army. But the Captain has already discredited himself, early in the play, by revealing his own greed and lack of idealism ("Mi pensar / ha de ser en procurar / de mejorar esta capa; / que suelen poco durar / aquestas guerras del papa" [I, 205-09]). So his exhortation to fame and glory is meant to be recognized as worthless. Not only is the sole statement on honor put in the mouth of a disreputable character, it is further discredited by a quarrel between two men precisely over the collection of salaries.

The argument between the soldiers Manrrique and Mendoça touches rapidly on all the sore spots of a Spaniard's existence. The practice of *desenterrar los muertos*, so bitterly denounced by Mateo Alemán, is vigorously exercised in the scene (III, 55-110). Manrrique cannot endure a *mentís* or imagined insult from Mendoça, drawing his sword and calling him a "puerco rremendón" (III, 74). Could this be a nasty reference to a previous identity as a *converso*, a previous occupation as a humble *ropero*? Mendoça in turn defends himself by making a sarcastic reference to the sexual potency of Manrrique's grandfather. Could this be a self-betraying sally, considering the *converso*'s contempt for the *villano*, whose sense of personal worth was rooted in his *machez*?[12] When Manrrique cuts deeper into Mendoça's uneasy identity ("Mas ¿de quándo, pese al cielo, / os llaman a vos Mendoça?" [III, 78-79]), we have a perfect example of the ironic failure of those who sought refuge in noble surnames—like Mendoça and Guzmán—which revealed far more than they concealed. The Captain and Guzmán, witnesses to these lacerating exchanges, intervene to separate the two men. The Captain, restraining Manrrique, tries to encourage a conciliatory handshake. Manrrique responds by shaking his fists, and Mendoça, held back by Guzmán, spits out a blunt "¡Cagá en ellas!" (III, 88). This is the kind of warfare that goes on in *Soldadesca*.

The quarrel between Mendoça and Manrrique is not the only quarrel in the play. The pandemonium that breaks out in front of the Italian Cola's inn, where several Spanish soldiers have been quartered, stands as the centerpiece of *Soldadesca*. The scene makes an eloquent statement of conflict and division. The soldiers do not speak Italian and Cola barely understands Spanish. A series of misunderstandings occur, the multilingual scene capturing the resentment that such forced lodgings caused among the people. More importantly, the scene captures the helplessness of the

---

[12] "La hombría sexual, la machez, como índice de la dimensión individual de la persona," Castro observed, invited typically *converso* attacks (*De la edad conflictiva* [Madrid: Taurus, 1961], p. 57, pp. 106-07, and *Hacia Cervantes*, tercera edición renovada [Madrid: Taurus, 1967], pp. 226 ff.).

invader, who is ravenously hungry and yet cannot even get a meal. The scene's uproarious hilarity should not distract us from its underlying sense of urgency and desperation. What emerge as the Spanish soldier's greatest enemies are hunger and the Italian language.

The scene also affords us a view of the invaders as seen through the eyes of an Italian: "Ay, uillani...marrani," Cola calls them (III, 255-56). This, significantly, is an insult learned from the Spaniards.[13] Cola's neighbor Joanfrancisco does a mocking imitation of the Spaniards: "Io tengo muchos dinieros / en las Cúrdubas, Sibilias; / míos patres caualieros / siñores de las Castilias" (III, 286-89). There is a remarkable refraction here: not only are we presented with a comic portrait of the Spaniards as seen by the Italians, but we find that the Spaniards are judged by the Italians according to a set of values learned from the Spaniards. Joanfrancisco's reaction is that of a Spanish *villano*, his outburst against the foreigners who presume to be the sons of "caualieros" betraying a peculiarly Spanish attitude. Interestingly, what most enrages Joanfrancisco about the Spaniards is precisely what an Old Christian would find enraging in a *converso*. The Italians, then, have learned to express their hatreds in curiously Spanish terms. How else are we to understand the following exchange?

COLA   ¿Qué dice questo marrano?
JUAN   ¿Tú no entiendes qué te digo,
        labrador y no villano?   (V, 52-54)

Juan's comic, excessively careful distinction between "labrador" and "villano" does not make sense unless we admit to the Spanish implications of each term. That an Old Christian, indeed a *labrador* such as Juan, should take pains not to provoke an Italian by referring to him as a *villano*, the way the *conversos* referred to the *gente menuda*, is very ironic. The exchange instantly recalls the complex social landscape that, while Spanish, endured in exile.

The climactic confrontation between Spaniards and Italians is followed by a contrasting, slower scene that has the feeling of

---

[13] "Porque los españoles despertaban un recelo, el de una ortodoxia insegura, debido a tantos judíos y marranos...la injuria de marrano se hizo popularísima contra los españoles en general" (Benedetto Croce, *España en la vida italiana durante el Renacimiento*, trans. J. Sánchez Rojas [Madrid: Mundo Latino, 1925], p. 184).

retreat from a lost fight into the world of private fantasy. The scene between Mendoça and Guzmán captures the frustration of men defeated by a lack of collective purpose, and by the warfare of daily existence. Mendoça proposes an escape, and soon the two men are launched into a series of sexual fantasies that threaten to provoke yet another quarrel. Along with the salaries that remain to be stolen, Guzmán wants to take along "vuestra amiga y la mía" (IV, 45). Mendoça is now inspired to take several more women. Guzmán expresses some doubt in their ability to find them, unless the women are "de almazén" (IV, 54). Mendoça's virility is suddenly at stake, and he protests his sexuality with a hyperbole ("Voto a Dios que van tras mí / seis dozenas más que bellas" [IV, 56-57]), which earns him Guzmán's stinging mockery ("Hermano, pues es ansí, / carguemos vn carro d'ellas" [IV, 58-59]). Guzmán averts a quarrel, swords drawn, by changing the topic: "que se quiere rrebolver / vna grandíssima guerra" (IV, 83-84).

Rumors of war in *Soldadesca* provide a fine example of history as perceived by the individual. As Guzmán whispers the highlights of the current political situation, Mendoça's mood slowly changes. He becomes exalted, and delivers a searing speech which, surprisingly, has been characterized as "irrelevant."[14] Mendoça expresses an awareness of the times, and of time itself as experienced by the individual, that is new and highly personal. Things are changing by the hour, and "Dios lo ordena / porque la gente desnuda / se vistan a costa ajena" (IV, 102-04). His is an ominous, even subversive voice, germane in tone to the rustic's in the *Introyto*. Mendoça then launches into a fantasy of what he would do "si duque o conde me viese" (IV, 143), evoking the image of the perfect *caballero*. Although the audience probably laughed at this quarrelsome, ragged Spaniard's pretensions, the truth is that Mendoça's vision recalls a better age. By implication, his speech is a disillusioned complaint about his own times, in which the spirit of *caritas* no longer exists. His dream evokes a false medieval past, yet the spirit that moves it suggests that of the new Christian humanist. Guzmán recognizes that there is a good measure of hopeless fantasy in Mendoça's evocation, and his "No os matéis" (IV, 165) is a sobering reply to what is probably Mendoça's most self-revealing moment in the play.

[14] Gillet, vol. IV, p. 506.

If alienation is what happens when the individual no longer
feels himself to be a part of the history of his generation, then all
the characters in *Soldadesca* are alienated. For what is alienation if
not the individual experience rendered unintelligible by the impos-
siblity of sharing in a collective vision of past and future? Zimic's
recent study on *Soldadesca* again deserves mention. Its thesis is that
the intent of the play is above all satirical. To be sure, Torres
Naharro does de-glorify the Spanish soldier, and the play does
trivialize the Spanish offensive in Italy. There is no doubt that
Soldadesca is an anti-war play. That in itself makes it an extraordinary work, a first in the history of the modern stage. Let us
remember that *Soldadesca* antecedes Erasmus' *Querella Pacis* (1517) by
a handful of years. But while a satiric intent is recognizable in the
play, we must also realize that Torres Naharro's portrayal of his
characters—Spaniards and Italians alike—is fundamentally sympathetic. Mendoça and Manrrique, Cola and Juan, Guzmán and the
rest all flicker before us in isolated moments of conflict and
rebellion, for life in *Soldadesca* is seen not as a continuum but as a
fragmented thing. Each character's anti-heroic gesture is a self-
revealing moment and not much else. Torres Naharro's purpose is
not only to censure the Spanish soldier in Italy, and to bemoan the
spectacle of Christians slaughtering each other in rival church-
men's wars. Torres Naharro expressed in *Soldadesca* his awareness
of life itself as warfare: daily warfare as perceived by the individual, for the enemy in the play is never made clear, unless it is a
world in shambles.

Torres Naharro, perhaps because of his own marginal situation
as a *converso*, invested each one of his characters with his own
disconcerted attitude towards the confusion, the displacement, the
fragmentation of his times.[15] More than a satire, *Soldadesca* is a

---

[15] "Su estilo mordaz," Castro observed, " . . . el modo 'intelectual' de
enfocar ciertas cuestiones, junto con otras circunstancias, parecen indicar
que Torres Naharro fue uno de tantos conversos del judaísmo que
hallaron refugio en Italia" (*La realidad histórica de España*, p. 185). For other
references to the dramatist's *converso* identity, see *De la edad conflictiva*, pp.
184-05, 207, 224, and *Hacia Cervantes*, pp. 127-28. Indeed, Torres Naharro
was probably a member of what Gilman calls "the first generation of
conversos to grow up under Inquisitional pressure" (*The Spain of Fernando de
Rojas*, p. 170). Also see Gilman, "Retratos de *conversos* en la *Comedia Jacinta*
de Torres Naharro," *Nueva Revista de Filología Hispánica*, 16 (1964), 20-39.

devastating indictment of the very history it is meant to exalt. The play captures the paradoxical phenomenon of human experience rendered valueless when "el tiempo se muda / d'ora en ora" (IV, 101-02), and it stands as a denial of history itself as a force that makes individual or collective human experience intelligible. Indeed, in a recent article Gilman cited *Soldadesca* as evidence of the *converso* artist's problematic relationship with the history of his generation.[16] Torres Naharro's play is a dubious monument to a history at once celebrated and debunked. What there is of affirmation in the play is each individual's claim to a world that once made sense; vertiginously changing times and the crumbling of a familiar social order render all such claims absurd. Is it any wonder, then, that the play ends with the cast marching offstage, a beggars' army evoking a false past with a song of courtly love, now no longer relevant and wrenchingly out of context?

NEW YORK CITY

---

[16] Stephen Gilman, "A Generation of Conversos," *Romance Philology,* 33 (1979-80), 98-99.

Poetry and History
in Gil Vicente's
Auto da Lusitânia

RONALD E. SURTZ

NATIVE OF PORTUGAL, Gil Vicente wrote plays in both Portuguese and Castilian for the bilingual Portuguese Court. Although he clearly participates in the flowering of theatrical activity initiated in Salamanca by Juan del Encina and Lucas Fernández in the late fifteenth century, his early plays so closely imitative of the Salamancans give way to experimentation with other dramatic formulas. While the *Auto da Lusitânia* has little formal resemblance to the pastoral plays of Encina and Fernández, it nonetheless shares with the Salamancan school the use of the theater to dramatize contemporary social and religious problems. Thus, the study of the *Auto* serves to illuminate the thematic preoccupations of the early peninsular theater.

The *Auto da Lusitânia* is a festival play first performed in 1532 to celebrate the birth of Prince Manuel of Portugal. The *auto* proper is a pseudo-Ovidian attempt to explain the mythological origins of certain Portuguese toponyms. The nymph Lisibea is loved by the Sun and gives birth to Lusitânia. Lusitânia, promised by her father to Mercury, the god of commerce, eventually weds the Greek prince Portugal, who requites her love. Jealous of her daughter, Lisibea dies and is buried on the site of the future city of Lisbon.

Gil Vicente, whose sources are essentially medieval, was criticized by certain humanists for his meager knowledge of classical learning. The *Auto da Lusitânia* has been interpreted as Gil Vicente's response to that criticism, i.e., as a parody of the efforts of Renaissance classicists to discover a Graeco-Roman origin or precedent for everything.[1] Gil Vicente's parodic approach forces the solar imagery of the place names, the Serra da Sintra with its Monte da Lua becoming Solercia. Lusitânia and her jealous mother quarrel in a manner ill-befitting the divine nature of the wife and daughter of the Sun. The goddesses Venus, Pallas, Rhea, and Juno pretend to have come from the East, just as, according to general belief in the sixteenth century, the gypsies came to Portugal from the East by way of Andalusia. Thus, in a parody of the hairsplitting scrupulosity in linguistic matters of certain humanists, the goddesses enter *ceceando* like gypsies.

The pseudo-mythological plot which forms the play proper is framed by what the Elizabethans would have called an induction, i.e., an introductory scene with multiple characters that develops a situation more or less complete in itself.[2] Gil Vicente's elaborate prologue consists of a series of genre-scenes depicting a Jewish tailor and his family. As Lediça, the tailor's daughter, sweeps the floor, she is courted by a Christian, who belongs to the nobility. Lediça will have nothing to do with her love-sick suitor, rejecting him with clever word-play. When the courtier claims to be burning up with great pain in his heart, Lediça says that she too has suffered from the same ailment. Doctor Aires told her it has to do with the spleen:

> CORTESÃO   Não falo, senhora, disso,
> porque eu me queimo e arço
> com dores de coração.

[1] Carolina Michaëlis de Vasconcelos, *Notas vicentinas* (Lisboa: Revista "Ocidente", 1949), p. 31. Gil Vicente makes fun of some of the matters treated by the humanists in his *Sermão* (1506): "No quiero arguir en placer ni pena, / los años de Arquiles, Patróculo *et cetra*, / ni desquadriñar allende de la letra, / si era mas luenga Ecuba o Elena. / Qué hace a la historia ser mala o buena / saber donde Ulises erró el camino? / Ni quiero ser cierto ni ser adivino, / quien fue el primer juez en Vaena." See his *Obras completas*, ed. Marques Braga, VI (Lisboa: Sá da Costa, 1944), p. 186. Future quotations from the Marques Braga edition will be indicated by the volume and page numbers in parentheses.

[2] See, for example, Thelma N. Greenfield, *The Induction in Elizabethan Drama* (Eugene: University of Oregon Press, 1969).

LEDIÇA Muitas vezes tenho eu isso:
diz Mestre Aires que é do baço,
e reina mais no Verão. (VI, 49)

The clever Lediça thus emblematically transfers the illness from
the heart, the seat of love and passion, to the spleen, the seat of
laughter.[3] When the courtier complains that his fate (*sorte*) has
condemned him to love, Lediça, intentionally misinterpreting *sorte*
as luck, warns her suitor against the evils of gambling:

CORTESÃO Mas, senhora, por amar
fiz minha sorte sujeita,
e perdi a mais andar.
LEDIÇA Crede, senhor, que o jogar
poicas vezes aproveita.
Dom Donegal Saborido,
que tinha tanta fazenda,
por jogar está perdido,
que não tem o dolorido
nem que compre nem que venda. (VI, 49-50)

They continue in this vein until the nobleman sees Lediça's father
approaching and makes his exit. The tailor sits down to attend to
his sewing, and the family members sing and chat as they work.
Two other Jews enter to announce the imminent arrival of the
royal family and suggest that all prepare an entertainment in
honor of the royal visit. The induction ends as the tailor advises
them to watch an *auto* by Gil Vicente to get some ideas for their
own presentation:

Pera que cumpridamente
aito novo inventemos
vejamos um excelente
que presente Gil Vicente,
e per hi nos regeremos. (VI, 63)

The induction and the *auto* it introduces do, of course, provide
an interesting example of Gil Vicente's manipulation of different
levels of reality. The spectators watch actors pretending to be

---

[3] Pliny the Elder noted, with reference to the spleen: "Sunt qui putent
adimi simul risum homini intemperantiamque eius constare lienis magni-
tudine." See Book XI, chapter 80, of his *Naturalis Historiae Libri XXXVII*, ed.
Carolus Mayhoff (Leipzig: Teubner, 1875), vol. II, p. 258.

spectators, who view a play given for members of the Portuguese royal family, who exist both as imaginary characters in the fictional world of the Jewish family and as "real" spectators in the audience viewing the play. But beyond the ludic teasing of the audience's perception of reality, certain thematic peculiarities in the induction, as well as that prologue's inordinate length (comprising as it does nearly a third of the entire performance), raise the question of what Gil Vicente hoped to achieve by introducing his mythological *auto* with such an elaborate and "realistic" prologue.

The answer to that question is, I believe, related to matters of chronology and to what we know of Gil Vicente outside of the literary world of his plays and poetry. The action of the induction is patently anachronistic, for in 1532 when the play was performed, there were theoretically no Jews in Portugal, the Portuguese Jews having been forced in 1497 to choose between expulsion and conversion to Christianity. Unlike the New Christians of Spain, where the Inquisition existed to watch over the sincerity of recent converts, the Portuguese New Christians were able to continue to practice their Judaism more or less openly, much to the alarm of the ecclesiastical authorities and to the resentment of the Old Christian populace. Such social tensions were manifested in the pogroms directed against the New Christians in 1506 and 1530. Finally, in 1531 King John of Portugal applied to the pope for the authorization necessary to establish an inquisition in Portugal, but the definitive bull that actually created the Portuguese Inquisition was not issued until 1536. Thus, in the year 1532 when the *Auto da Lusitânia* was first performed, the establishment of the Inquisition was not yet a *fait accompli,* and the charming and sympathetic portrait of the Jewish family in the induction could be interpreted as a plea for tolerance.

Such a hypothesis is plausible in the light of what we know of Gil Vicente's other efforts on behalf of the Portuguese New Christians. When an earthquake struck Santarém in 1531, the Old Christian populace, aroused by the preaching of certain friars, claimed that God had wished to punish the New Christians for their Judaizing. Vicente did not agree with such an interpretation and in a speech to the friars he argued that such disasters are not manifestations of the wrath of God, but rather a part of the natural order of things in the sublunar world in which all matter is eventually reduced to its prime state:

E porque nenhuma cousa há hi debaixo do sol sem tornar a ser o
que foi, e o que viram dêsta qualidade de tremor havia de tornar
a ser por força, ou cedo ou tarde, não o escreveram. Concruo
que não foi este nosso espantoso tremor, *ira Dei;*... (VI, 253)

The earthquake, therefore, had nothing to do with the religious
practices of the New Christians. The tolerant attitude apparent in
the induction of the *Auto da Lusitânia* is thus an evident reflection of
one of the few records we have of Gil Vicente's official views on
the subject (or on any other subject, for that matter).[4]

The play proper had probably been composed before the birth
of Prince Manuel. Meanwhile, an outbreak of the plague in Lisbon
forced the royal family to flee the city, and the Prince was born in
the town of Alvito. But the performance of Vicente's play was
postponed, possibly due to fear of contagion if additional actors
(there are 22 roles in the play) had to be brought in from Lisbon.
In any case the play was not performed until the return of the
court to Lisbon in the summer of 1532, for which performance
Vicente added the induction.[5] It is significant to note that between
the birth of Prince Manuel in November of 1531 and the actual
performance of the play, the pope authorized the establishment of
the Portuguese Inquisition (December 17, 1531), the first Inquisi-
tor General was named (January 13, 1532), and a law was enacted
(June 14, 1532) that forbade the New Christians to leave Portugal.[6] Such a law was, of course, a sure indication of the progress of
the secret negotiations that would result in the definitive establishment of an inquisition in Portugal (papal bull of May 23, 1536).
Whether the induction of the *Auto da Lusitânia* was an already-
composed fragment adapted to the occasion or a newly-written
piece, it is evident that Gil Vicente consciously linked the induction
to the birthday play as propaganda reflecting his current interest in
the fate of the Portuguese New Christians. It is for this reason

---

[4] Earlier, in his *Sermão* of 1506 Gil Vicente alluded with disapproval to
the forced conversions of 1497: "Es por demas pedir al judio/que sea
cristiano en su corazon; /... Também está llano/que es por demas al que
es mal cristiano/doctrina de Cristo por fuerza ni ruego" (VI, 195).

[5] Oscar de Pratt, *Gil Vicente. Notas e comentários* (Lisboa: Teixeira, 1931),
pp. 254-55.

[6] For the chronology see Alexandre Herculano, *Obras completas. História
da origem e estabelecimento da Inquisição em Portugal,* revisão de Vitorino Nemésio
(Amadora: Livraria Bertrand, 1975), I, pp. 222-39.

that the induction is intended to refer to the historical circumstances of its performance and not necessarily to the play it introduces.

And yet, beyond the apparent lack of connection between induction and play, there are certain parallels which at least suggest a unity of sorts. The play as a whole can be viewed as revolving around the notion of love. On an explicit level love is manifested through the social ritual of courtship. Lediça is courted by her nobleman in the induction, as Lusitânia is courted by both Mercury and Portugal in the play proper. On an implicit level love is manifested through a plea for charity. Gil Vicente asks his audience to adopt an attitude of tolerance towards the New Christians and to accept his lack of humanistic erudition as in no way detracting from his literary abilities.[7]

And just as the play proper concerns a going back in time to discover the "true" origins of Lisbon, the induction uses a similar technique to present the New Christians in a favorable light. Although the time of the induction turns out to coincide with the arrival of the royal family in Lisbon in the summer of 1532, Gil Vicente purposely makes the initial episodes appear to take place at the end of the fifteenth century when Portuguese Jews and Christians lived in relative harmony.[8] Thus, Lediça claims to be a good

---

[7] His prologuist recites a fanciful biography of Gil Vicente (VI, 64-66). Grandson of a tamborine-player, son of a midwife and a maker of packsaddles, Vicente was carried off by a devil disguised as a damsel to the cave of the sibyl where he learned of the mythical origins of Portugal. Perhaps the Portuguese humanists viewed Gil Vicente as coming from such lowly origins, both biologically and spiritually. By anticipating such a negative viewpoint and by presenting himself in an intentionally unglamorous light, Vicente negates the humanist perception by the very outrageousness of his self-portrait. As a final "dig" at the proponents of the new learning, Vicente adds the pseudo-classical visit to the sibylline cave to his biography. His burlesque self-portrait thus dramatizes his preoccupations as an author. He asks his audience to recognize, as he himself does, that his genius lies with the old learning, not with the new.

[8] Francisco Márquez Villanueva observes a similar anachronism in the case of Vicente's Farsa de Inês Pereira: "Representada (según su rúbrica) ante Juan III en 1523, la Farsa de Inêz Pereira atestigua todavía acerca de una convivencia fácil entre cristianos y judíos que, si no era reflejo exacto de la realidad social del momento, da obvia fe de un pasado muy inmediato para todos y que el autor contempla con cariñosa mirada." See his "'Os judeus

friend of Isaac Abravanel and of Abraham Zacut, who left Portu-
ʲgal in 1483 and 1496 respectively.[9] Moreover, the required participation of Jews in royal entries is a typically medieval phenome-
ʲnon.[10]

Gil Vicente's art is one of juxtaposition. Acting in defense of his
artistic integrity, the playwright attempts to out-humanist the
humanists by constructing a pseudo-mythological plot as far-
fetched as any they might imagine, albeit a parody whose very
implausibility is an indirect attack on the extremes of what often
passed for classical scholarship in the Renaissance. To the ultimately self-destructive implausibility of the play proper is juxta-

casamenteiros' de Gil Vicente," in *Les Cultures ibériques en devenir. Essais publiés
en hommage à la mémoire de Marcel Bataillon* (Paris: Fondation Singer-Polignac,
1979), p. 377.

[9] In the introduction to his commentary on the Book of Joshua, Isaac
Abravanel spoke of the favor he enjoyed under Afonso V of Portugal: "I
lived in peace in my inherited house in the renowned city of Lisbon, the
capital of Portugal, where God had given me blessings, riches and honor
.... I was beloved in the palace of Alfonso, a just and mighty king, under
whom the Jews enjoyed liberty and prosperity." Quoted in Jacob S.
Minkin, *Abarbanel and the Expulsion of the Jews from Spain* (New York: Behr-
man's Jewish Book House, 1938), p. 67.

[10] The Jews regularly participated in Portuguese royal entries. In a
letter of 1402, King John I observes that "des pouco tempo a cá os Judeos
das Cõmunas das Cidades, Villas, e Lugares do nosso Senhorio quando
saem fora dos lugares, honde Cõmunas de Judeos ha, receber com trebe-
lhos a nós...." See *Ordenaçoens do Senhor Rey D. Affonso V* (Coimbra, 1792),
Livro II, Título 75, p. 451. In 1450 Jews participated in the festivities
honoring the marriage of Leonor, sister of Afonso V of Portugal, to
Frederick III of Germany. See A. H. de Oliveira Marques, *A sociedade
medieval portuguesa,* 3ª edição (Lisboa: Sá da Costa, 1974), p. 207. Vicente's
nostalgia for his nation's medieval past before all was changed by the
overseas enterprises is echoed in several episodes in the play. Lusitânia
rejects the cold god of commerce in favor of the loving and chivalrous
Portugal. Ninguém, dressed as a pauper, confronts Todo o Mundo,
dressed, significantly, "como rico mercador." Through the report prepared
for Lucifer by two devils, Vicente expresses his criticism of contemporary
morals: "Que Ninguém busca consciêcia, e Todo o Mundo dinheiro. / ...
que busca honra Todo o Mundo, / e Ninguém busca virtude," etc. (VI, 84-
85). And even the Jewish tailor dreams of going off to fight the Moors (VI,
60-61). In other plays Vicente expresses a similar disconformity with the
changes wrought in Portuguese society as its economy evolved from an
agricultural base to one concentrated on colonial trade.

posed the more positive *in illo tempore* of the anachronistic portrait of the Portuguese Jews. Thus, induction and play proper constitute a parallel plea for tolerance towards the New Christians as human beings and for tolerance towards Gil Vicente as an artist.[11]

PRINCETON UNIVERSITY

[11] A preliminary version of this study was read at the Modern Language Association Convention, December, 1978.

The Unity of
La gran Semíramis
of Cristóbal de Virués

JAMES CRAPOTTA

LTHOUGH THE EARLY sixteenth century witnes-
sed a new departure in the Spanish theater,
it is not until the last quarter of that century
that we can speak of a Spanish tragedy intended for public performance.[1] Dramatists
such as Jerónimo de Bermúdez, Leonardo
Lupercio de Argensola, Juan de la Cueva,
Cristóbal de Virués, and even Cervantes
were each trying to create dramas that would both entertain and
edify, and for this purpose they turned to the theater of Seneca—
sometimes directly, sometimes via Italian neo-Senecan dramatists
such as Giraldi Cinthio—for inspiration. However, this shared
aspiration of popularizing a noble and moralizing dramatic theater
did not preclude individual, and even experimental, approaches to
both dramatic form and content. One only need recall Cueva's
appropriation of medieval Spanish legends, or Cervantes' attempt
in *Numancia* to make his countrymen aware of their own classical
history to realize that the *tragedia* in the hands of these authors
adhered to no rigid classical pattern. Instead, it was a rather

---

[1] For a discussion of sixteenth-century Spanish tragedy, see Alfredo
Hermenegildo, *La tragedia en el Renacimiento español* (Barcelona: Planeta,
1973).

49

loosely defined and eminently flexible form and, as such, it helped pave the way for the triumphant *comedia*.

Among these "trágicos españoles" Virués stands out as one of the most important precursors of Lope. In both his *Arte nuevo de hacer comedias* and *Laurel de Apolo* Lope acknowledges the theater's debt to Virués.[2] In an important study, William C. Atkinson has shown how Virués anticipates the practice of Lope in his adaptation of varied meters (including the first use of *romance* in the theater) to conform to plot situation, his free use of novelistic elements, his reduction of the number of acts to three, his use of subplots, and his use of Spanish settings in the later plays.[3]

But Virués also shares with Lope a consciousness of the need to create a "modern" theater. His works, from the sober tragedy of *Elisa Dido* to the quasi-romantic comedy of *La infelice Marcela*, reveal an author eager to expand the potential of the *tragedia* so as to please a contemporary audience. In this essay I shall discuss how in his play *La gran Semíramis* Virués explores a new approach to tragedy. It is a work which depicts not a single, linear action but rather a series of parallel and interconnected actions which illustrate a common theme.[4]

---

2   El Capitán Virués, insigne ingenio,
     puso en tres actos la Comedia, que antes
     andava en cuatro, como pies de niño,
     que eran entonces niñas las comedias.
                    (*Arte nuevo*, vv. 215-18.)

     ¡O ingenio singular! en paz reposa,
     a quien las Musas Cómicas debieron
     los mejores principios que tuvieron.
                    (*Laurel de Apolo*, silva IV.)

3 William C. Atkinson, "Seneca, Virués, Lope de Vega," in *Homenatge a Antoni Rubió i Lluch* (Barcelona: 1936), I, 111-31. See also Rinaldo Froldi, *Lope de Vega y la formación de la comedia* (Madrid: Anaya, 1973), pp. 110-15.

4 The following is a brief summary of the action of *La gran Semíramis*: *Act I*: King Nino of Assyria is attempting to capture the city of Batra but the city remains well defended by the troops of Alexandro. Semíramis, wife of Nino's chief general, Menón, unexpectedly arrives to join her husband. She is disguised as a man. She suggests a new strategy for gaining access to the city, which is carried out successfully. Attracted by both the beauty and the military astuteness of Menón's wife, Nino orders his general to cede her to him. Menón refuses and Nino abducts Semíra-

That Virués was attempting to break new ground in dramatic structure is evident in the prologue to this play where he proclaims himself an innovator:

> ... advierto
> que esta tragedia, con estilo nuevo
> que ella introduze, viene en tres jornadas
> que suceden en tiempos diferentes:
> en el sitio de Batra la primera,
> en Nínive famosa la segunda,
> la tercera y final en Babilonia.
> Formando en cada cual una tragedia
> con que podrá toda la de [h]oi tenerse
> por tres tragedias, no sin arte escritas.
> Ni es menor novedad que la que dixe
> de ser primera en ser de tres jornadas. (25b-26a)[5]

And in the prologue to the 1609 edition of his works he describes himself as a playwright who combines innovation with a certain respect for tradition. He wrote four of these plays, he says,

> ... aviendo procurado juntar en ellas lo mejor del arte antiguo i de la moderna costumbre, con tal concierto i tal atención a todo

mis with only minimal protest on her part. In despair, Menón hangs himself.

Act II: Several years have passed. In the city of Nínive Nino grants Semíramis, now his wife, five days of independent rule. Taking advantage of the situation, she has Nino imprisoned and her look-alike son, Ninias, assume his mother's attire and retire to live as a Vestal Virgin. Semíramis, now disguised as Ninias, reads a letter to the governing council describing how Nino was assumed into Heaven and how Semíramis is retiring from public life in favor of Ninias. Still disguised, she has Nino brought before her. Believing his wife murdered by their son, Nino drinks poison. Before he dies Semíramis reveals the truth to him.

Act III: Having ruled successfully for six years, Semíramis discloses her real identity and proclaims the real Ninias king. Her incestuous desire for her son arouses his disgust and Ninias kills his mother. He persuades the council that Semíramis has ascended into Heaven in the form of a dove. He then privately orders the disposal of her body.

5 All quotations from the play are from the edition of Eduardo Juliá Martínez, *Poetas dramáticos valencianos* (Madrid: Tipografía de la "Revista de Archivos", 1929), I. The numerals and letters in parentheses refer to page and column respectively.

lo que se deve tener, que parece que llegan al punto de lo que en
las obras del teatro en nuestros tiempos se devría usar.[6]

Thus, his aim is neither to destroy totally classical dramatic form
nor be its slave but rather to create a type of tragedy appropriate
to the audience of his own time.[7] This would entail not a rupture
with the past, but a compromise with it. In the *Semíramis* prologue
his bold affirmation of an "estilo nuevo" is tempered with the
assurance that this novelty does not set out to violate the time-
honored rules of Art ("no sin arte escritas").

In his description of this play Virués makes explicit his rejection
of the Aristotelian unities by drawing attention to the fact that the
play occurs in three different periods of time, in three distinct
settings, and consists of three tragedies. The play, then, may be
seen as depicting both three distinct "actions" and a single one at
the same time. On one hand, each act taken as a self-contained
entity is a perfectly structured "classical" tragedy which takes place
within twenty-four hours, remains in a single geographic location,
and focuses on the fall of one figure. On the other hand, each act
contributes an incident to a single drama, sprawling in time and
space, whose subject is "la vida y muerte de la gran Semíramis"
(25b). Thus, one way in which Virués comes to terms with the
classical precepts is by honoring them within the component parts
of the play while discarding them in the overall structure. Here too
Virués may have paved the way for Lope. It is perhaps not
insignificant that in his *Arte nuevo*, in the verses that immediately
precede an acknowledgment of Virués as the father of the three-
act play in Spain, Lope prescribes the following formula for divid-
ing the action of the *comedia:*

> El sujeto escriba en prosa,
> y en tres actos de tiempo le reparta
> procurando, si pueda, en cada uno
> no interrumpir el término del día. (vv. 211-14)

The real art of Virués consists of his ability to reduce the

---

[6] Cited in Eduardo Juliá Martínez, "Observaciones preliminares" to
Poetas dramáticos valencianos, I, lii-liii.

[7] Lope, too, registers his concern with writing for a contemporary
audience in the very title of his *Arte nuevo: Arte nuevo de hacer comedias en este
tiempo.*

wealth of narrative detail found in his sources, the *Bibliotheca Historica* of Diodorus Siculus and the *Epitoma Historiarum Philippicarum* of Justin,[8] and shape it into three parallelly structured and intimately interconnected tragedies, each of which illustrates a single unifying theme: how uncontrolled erotic passion leads to self-disintegration and, hence, to a fall from Fortune. For all their diversity of action, all three acts share the following basic structure:

1. Each presents a character—Menón in the first act, Nino in the second, Semíramis in the third—at the height of Fortune;
2. This character falls victim to an overwhelming erotic passion;
3. This uncontrolled passion sets in motion a process of self-disintegration as each character cedes his authority and, hence, his very identity to the beloved; this step is signaled by a disguise or a change of clothing;
4. Each meets a violent death which hovers somewhere between murder and suicide;
5. His body is removed from the stage by courtiers, signalling the fall from Fortune and the beginning of a new cycle of power.

However, these are not merely what might be called *tragedias paralelas*, but *tragedias encadenadas* as well. Each tragedy grows organically out of the preceding one. Virués achieves this first of all, and most obviously, by turning the victor of one act into the victim of the next. Thus, in the first act Alexandro is defeated by Menón,[9] who is in turn victimized by Nino; in the second Nino is mistreated by Semíramis; and in the third Semíramis is killed by her son. And just as the death of Alexandro suggests a tragedy prior to those presented on stage, so Virués intimates that Ninias, the mirror image of his mother, will continue the cycle of rises and falls once the last act has ended.

The second manner in which the three acts are interwoven is that each new death takes over a specific detail of the previous one

[8] For Virués' sources see Cecilia Vennard Sargent, *A Study of the Dramatic Works of Cristóbal de Virués* (New York: Hispanic Institute of the United States, 1930), and Pedro Calderón de la Barca, *La hija del aire*, ed. Gwynne Edwards (London: Tamesis, 1970), pp. xxiii-xxxiv.

[9] Although Alexandro is defeated by the plan of Semíramis, it is Menón who identifies himself as the victor.

and either expands on it or comments on it ironically. The first set of interconnected fates is that of Menón and the enemy general Alexandro. After the defeat of his troops by the Assyrian forces, Alexandro hangs himself. Later, Menón discovers his body and carries the rope on stage. For him the rope serves as a visible sign of the cruel instability of Fortune:

> Esta es la soga que quité al cuitado,
> que la traxe comigo para exemplo
> de los crueles casos de Fortuna. (32a)

Soon thereafter, in despair over Nino's abduction of his wife, Menón hangs himself with that very rope. He sees his own life as yet another *caso de fortuna*. In Menón's eyes Nino comes to represent the generic tyrant who, like Fortune, turns unexpectedly cruel, and he exhorts soldiers, courtiers and all those who hope to attain worldly glory by following "estos tiranos" (34a) to learn from his example the transient nature of all the world has to offer.

But if Menón would have us equate his plight with that of Alexandro, Virués exploits the obvious parallel of their suicides in an ironic fashion. The repeated elements that seem to link their deaths—the rope, the appeal to inconstant Fortune—serve instead to underline the enormous moral distance which separates their lives and, in so doing, illuminate the theme of the disintegrating power of uncontrolled passion. Alexandro may have been defeated in battle, but his suicide, like that of the people of Numancia, represents an act of defiance. In taking his own life he declares an unwillingness to diminish his sense of honor as a man and as a warrior by submitting to captivity. Thus, Nino comments of him:

> También quiso mostrarnos Alexandro
> su furor diabólico en la muerte,
> como en la vida justa paga tiene
> de sus soberbios i arrogantes hechos. (32a)

Menón's death, however, reveals no such sense of honor. If Alexandro's noble death is a mirror of his "soberbios i arrogantes hechos," so is Menón's ultimate act of despair a reflection of the dishonor and false illusions that constitute the fabric of his life. At the very opening of the play Menón tells the audience that his love for his wife stands above his honor, for he has abandoned the battlefield to be by her side:

Arremetía ya el abierto muro,
puestos los ojos en la gloria i fama;
pero sabiendo que llegastes,
juro que me traxo volando a vos mi llama,
i aunque el [h]onor viniendo me aventuro,
verá quien me juzgare, si me infama,
que importa más gozar de vos, mi cielo,
que quanta gloria puede darme el suelo.   (26a)

As John G. Weiger has observed, these lines indicate that, from the very outset of the act, Menón is "on the road to self-extinction."[10] The love which he places at the center of his world is far from virtuous, even though his union with Semíramis is sanctioned by marriage. Instead, it partakes of three ignoble qualities which will characterize all the amorous passions represented in the play. First of all, it is not a spiritual, ennobling love, but a physical, lustful passion; twice in the opening scene he states that his only desire in life is to "gozar de vos" (26a, 26b). Second, it is narcissistic; he tells his wife that he would have welcomed death,

si no esperara verme en essos ojos
que convierten en glorias mis enojos.   (26b)

Finally, it confuses the divine with the merely human; he refers to the object of his love as "mi cielo" (26a) and "divino espíritu" (27b). Later, when Nino demands that he cede his wife to his king, Menón's words strangely parody those of a Christian martyr who refuses to abandon his faith; he will oppose the will of his monarch even if threatened by Heaven itself with eternal damnation:

I digo que aunque el cielo me atormente
con sus mayores fuerças y tormentos
i tú, señor, airado e inclemente
prueves en mí mil fieros pensamientos,
i aunque me abrase el fuego eterno ardiente
i un caos hagan de mí los elementos,
i aunque vuelva a no ser, que es mayor mengua,
no podrá dar tal sí jamás mi lengua.   (32b)

The result of this misguided, blinding passion is that it strips Menón of his masculinity and his identity as an honorable man.

---

[10] John G. Weiger, *The Valencian Dramatists of Spain's Golden Age* (Boston: Twayne, 1976), p. 35.

Menón, the "segunda persona del gran Nino" (27a), hands over his role of conquering general to his wife, who leads the forces of Nino to victory while dressed as a man. That reversal of roles is reflected in their speech, for while Semíramis speaks of war, Menón is interested only in love.[11]

Menón's willing abdication of his identity as a man causes him to lose his place of privilege in his society. King Nino is about to honor Menón for his victory when he discovers that this distinction is due Semíramis instead. At the very moment when attention should have been focused on Menón it is shifted to his wife. Admiration and lust are awakened in the king at the same time. Menón, then, bears direct responsibility for his fall. It is his uncontrolled passion for his wife which unsettles his sense of values and diminishes his worth in the eyes of his monarch.

Returning to his death soliloquy, we have seen that Menón claims he is imitating Alexandro in choosing death over life. But his belief that he has reached a state of *desengaño*, that he now understands that life offers no certainty, is undercut ironically by his own words, for he is no closer to discerning truth in his moment of death than he was in life. If his words reverberate with Stoic commonplaces, he nonetheless believes that his wife has been assumed into Heaven and he calls to her to take him away with her. If Alexandro could not live without honor, Menón cannot live without his wife, a woman who, far from heavenly, has just betrayed him by assenting to her own abduction.[12] Menón's death may indeed teach us—as he himself claims—that earthly rulers are not to be trusted, but it also demonstrates that man is infinitely capable of self-deceit. Although Nino provokes

---

[11] MENÓN: I vos, dulce Semíramis, querida,
               al coraçón que en fuego se resuelve
               i en él, cual Fénis, halla nueva vida,
               mientras vuestro valor i ser rebuelve
               dalde en vuestra alma alvergue i acogida,
               para que entienda della las grandezas
               i goze sus tesoros i riquezas.
                  . . . .
         SEMÍRAMIS: Tengo [vuest]ra alma en mí i por esso acierto. (27b)

[12] For a discussion of the "elocuente silencio" of Semíramis, see John G. Weiger, *Hacia la comedia: De los valencianos a Lope* (Madrid: Cupsa, 1978), p. 82.

the tragic crisis by turning against his general, Menón's death is ultimately an act of suicide. As such, it is an appropriately symbolic end for a man who has willingly surrendered his masculine integrity, and hence his very being, to another in succumbing to erotic passion.

In the second act it is the ambition of Semíramis which seems to set the Wheel of Fortune turning. Upon seeing Nino betrayed by his queen, the courtier Zopiro laments:

> ¡Oh, fortuna! ¿[H]ai cosa igual
> en ligereza a tu rueda?
> . . . .
>
> Ayer fue Nino un Monarca
> i alcançó a serlo en el mundo
> . . . .
>
> i es [h]oy un triste cautivo. (41a)

But here too passion is the catalyst of the tragic fall. As in the case of Menón, Nino's surrender to love leads to disintegration and a loss of personal identity. Already in the first act, the king wishes he were not himself so that he could enjoy the favors of Semíramis:

> No fuera Nino Menón,
> aunque Menón fuera Nino. (30b)

Similarly, he is all too ready to relinquish his social identity as king. Rather than rule, he prefers to be ruled by Love:

> . . . le fuerça
> al rei otro rei mayor
> i en su pretensión se esfuerça
> ques el poderoso Amor,
> contra quien ni [h]ai lei ni fuerça. (31a)

When the second act begins, Nino's words could well be those of Menón, for he cedes everything to Semíramis:

> Siempre te amé con este amor ardiente;
> siempre mi voluntad, gozo i desseo
> fue tu contento i gozo solamente;
>   tus ojos son la luz con que yo veo;
> tu alma, como a ti, me da a mí vida;
> tu gloria sola es la que yo desseo. (36a)

Like his general, Nino abdicates his responsibilities to his beloved. He assents to her request that she be allowed to occupy the
throne and rule in his stead for five days. His delight in seeing his
wife holding the symbols of royal power recalls the narcissism of
Menón:

> Sentaos, Reina i señora, en este asiento
> que es dedicado a la Real persona;
> tomá este cetro, i seaos ornamento
> de verdadera Reina esta corona;
> con ecesivo amor, gozo i contento
> de su mano el gran Nino aquí os corona. (37a)

This "ecesivo amor" of which Nino speaks has clouded over his
reason so that he hands over his power, and hence, his identity, to
another. His words imply another reversal of roles: he sees with
her eyes, while she sits on *his* throne. The second act of *La gran
Semíramis*, then, is not merely about ambition. Given the corruption
of the royal court, the queen could have killed her husband at any
time. The fact that this occurs only after the king allows her to
rule in his place indicates that Virués sought to emphasize theme
over arbitrary action. What matters is not so much that Semíramis
kills Nino as that she can take control only when the king ceases to
be himself.

The death of Nino plays on the audience's recollection of the
end of the previous act. If Nino is brutalized by his wife's hench-
men, it is he who takes his own life under the false assumption
that she is dead. He too believes that she inhabits the celestial
spheres and expects to join her there. But Nino's death is more
horrible than that of Menón, for he is denied the consolation of his
own illusion: just as he is about to expire, Semíramis reveals the
awful truth.

The relationship between erotic passion and the loss of identity
reaches its culmination in the last act. The fall from Fortune of
Semíramis is unequivocally linked to her inability to subjugate her
own passions and appetites:

> [h]a sido rei i capitán famoso,
> alcançando vitorias i trofeos
> de todos sus contrarios, sino solo
> de aquellos que consigo el [h]ombre trae,
> que son los viles apetitos ciegos,
> de quien [h]a sido siempre avassallada. (55a)

For six years she has ruled and conquered dressed as a man. Now she has decided to reveal herself as a woman and to return the throne to her son, Zameis Ninias. In a play of repeated changes of identity where nothing is what it seems to be, this apparent return to order—where a woman is acknowledged as a woman, and a man as a man—must of necessity be deemed suspect.

If Semíramis has attained a privileged position, it is *as a man* that she has triumphed, and the return to her female identity must be viewed as a betrayal of her masculine personality. Like her predecessors she is undone by Eros. Her total submission to the beloved and subsequent loss of identity is strongly underscored by the absolute physical resemblance between mother and son. Her love for her son, who in royal garb cannot be distinguished from his mother when she was dressed as a man, is at once the ultimate act of narcissism and of the negation of selfhood. Once she cedes the throne, she ceases to be what and who she is. The celebrated conqueror now kneels prostrate before her son.

It is only now that she no longer has control of herself that she is vulnerable, for it is his disgust over her love for him that causes Ninias to turn against his mother. Her death scene is set off against that of Nino. While Nino took his life because he was convinced that Ninias had killed Semíramis, in the third act this lie becomes a reality. But the death of Semíramis is not simply matricide. The remarkable physical resemblance of the murderer and his victim strongly suggests that, at some level, Semíramis has taken her own life as had both Menón and Nino. Thus, there is a suggestion of suicide in Ninias' murder of his mother, which in turn implies a repetition of the cycle.

Indeed, Semíramis' real incarnation is in her son who, far from restoring order, promises to continue his mother's reign of deception. Just as she had invented the tale of Nino's assumption into Heaven to deceive the Assyrians, so too her son now invents the tale of her assumption to Heaven in the shape of a dove. These deceptions, and the revelation that Semíramis was the daughter of a prostitute, are a final ironic commentary on the false illusions that caused Menón and Nino to take their own lives. Ninias' deceptions portend his own fall. As the courtier Diarco informs us: "En cuerpo i alma todo es cual su madre" (57a).

If the very personal dramatic formula represented by *La gran Semíramis* was not to be repeated, not even by Virués himself, the play nonetheless anticipates the future *comedia* in two important ways. First, it helped train the audience to seek out important thematic relationships and, ultimately, a thematic unity. As A.A. Parker has pointed out, the pre-eminence of theme over action was to be an important principle of the *comedia*.[13] Second, in terms of the values presented to the audience, *La gran Semíramis* teaches that submission to uncontrolled passion leads to the disintegration of not only the personal self, but also the social self. Central to the play is the lesson that one's being is intimately bound with one's social role. Menón, Nino, and Semíramis cease to be *who* they are at the very moment that they abdicate their social responsibilities, that is, at the very moment they cease to be *what* they are. It would not be long before this notion would become the credo-like formula *soy quien soy*, so central to the social ideology of the *comedia*.

BARNARD COLLEGE

[13] A. A. Parker, "The Approach to the Spanish Drama of the Golden Age," *Tulane Drama Review*, 4 (1959), 42-59. The importance of Virués in this area is noted by Gwynne Edwards: "... Virués' significant contribution ... was one of organizing and reshaping something loose and episodic in order to develop certain themes. In this respect he is a clear forerunner of the great Golden Age dramatists ..." (Gwynne Edwards, "Calderón's *La hija del aire* in the Light of his Sources," *Bulletin of Hispanic Studies*, 43 [1966], 184).

Authors, Characters, and Readers in *Grimalte y Gradissa*

BARBARA F. WEISSBERGER

THE SALAMANCA OF Fernando de Rojas was not only an intellectual haven, not only a milieu of intense historical innovation; it also represented what, in more than one way, was the highest cultural level ever reached by an oral society. The printing press had not yet diluted or blurred the edges of language. Nor had it yet created a public capable of limiting literary creation by habitual expectations.... But it had, in the two decades of its effective existence in Spain, multiplied many times the possibilities of literary experience. Even more it had given that very important kind of experience an intensity, a sense of novelty, and a sudden self-consciousness which it had hardly possessed before.

The Spain of Fernando de Rojas

TEPHEN GILMAN'S equating of the much-discussed "transitional" nature of *La Celestina* with the change from an oral culture to a print culture in Spain greatly advances our understanding of the genesis of Rojas' masterpiece.[1] At the same time it opens up new avenues of investigation for those of us interested in the flowering of Spanish romance that also took place in that crucial final decade of the fifteenth century. It is the purpose of this essay to follow that investigative path as it applies to one romance of the period, Juan de Flores' *Grimalte y Gradissa*.

[1] Stephen Gilman, *The Spain of Fernando de Rojas* (Princeton: Princeton University Press, 1972), pp. 310-35.

In his consideration of *Celestina* as the reflection of a
sophisticated oral-aural culture in the process of being drastically
and permanently altered by the printing press, Gilman briefly
mentions the role of the *novela sentimental* in that transformation.[2]
He refers specifically to the publishing history of Diego de San
Pedro's sentimental romances, *Tractado de amores de Arnalte y Lucenda*
and *Cárcel de Amor*. Although San Pedro's two works were
published only one year apart, in 1491 and 1492 respectively,
scholars have established that *Arnalte* was actually written years
prior to its appearance in print (probably between 1479 and 1482),
and that many years intervened before San Pedro composed
Cárcel.[3] But it remained for Gilman to hypothesize that what
stimulated San Pedro to write a second romance—and one that
adheres closely to the first in content and, somewhat less so, in
structure as well—was in fact the immediate success of his first
published work. *Cárcel de Amor* would, under these circumstances,
hold the distinction of being "the first novel written for the
printing press . . . an event at least as significant to the sociology of
Spanish literature as that of the *Amadís*."[4]

  [2] Gilman credits Marshall McLuhan's *The Gutenberg Galaxy* (Toronto:
Toronto University Press, 1962) with stimulating, in part, his discussion
of *Celestina* and of the rise of print culture in Spain. A rereading of Gilman
and McLuhan did much to shape the present essay. For a broader
understanding of the role of typography in the evolution of human
consciousness, the following works of Walter Ong are indispensable: *The
Presence of the Word* (New Haven: Yale University Press, 1967); *Rhetoric,
Romance, and Technology* (Ithaca: Cornell University Press, 1971); and *Interfaces of the Word* (Ithaca: Cornell University Press, 1977).

  [3] Samuel Gili Gaya in the Introduction to his edition of San Pedro's
Obras (Clásicos Castellanos, 133, 3rd edition [Madrid: Espasa-Calpe,
1967], pp. xxii-xxxi) first posited the time lapse between the composition
of the two works. The more precise dating was arrived at by Keith
Whinnom in the Introduction to vol. I of his *Obras completas* of San Pedro
(Clásicos Castalia, 54 [Madrid: Castalia, 1973], 44-46). For additional
evidence in support of that lapse, based on the change in San Pedro's
attitude toward the policies of Ferdinand and Isabella that is evinced in
Cárcel, see Francisco Márquez Villanueva, "*Cárcel de Amor*: novela política,"
Revista de Occidente, 4 (1966), 185-200, rpt. in F. Márquez Villanueva,
Relecciones de literatura medieval (Sevilla: Publicaciones de la Universidad de
Sevilla, 1977), pp. 75-94.

  [4] Gilman, *Spain*, pp. 327-28, n. 125. As far as I know, the only other
scholar to come close to making this point is Alan Deyermond in *A*

One cannot, to be sure, assume from this that San Pedro was writing exclusively for a public of silent readers. *Cárcel* no less than *Celestina* was still primarily read aloud in groups. The transition from an oral culture to a visual and technological one was very gradual in Spain, as elsewhere in Europe.[5] Nevertheless, one aspect of *Cárcel* supports the contention that San Pedro incorporated into his second romance an understanding of the difference between the oral and the written experience of literature. I am referring to the considerable simplification of style that is evident in *Cárcel*, as compared to *Arnalte*.

The first critic to remark the significant difference between the styles of *Arnalte* and *Cárcel* was Samuel Gili Gaya, but we owe the detailed analysis of San Pedro's stylistic reform to Keith Whinnom. He has shown that the changes introduced into *Cárcel* consist chiefly in the abandonment of the many acoustic conceits and the rhymed prose characteristic of the earlier work, and in a new concern with the techniques of *abbreviatio*. Whinnom attributes such changes solely to the influence on San Pedro, a writer closely associated with the court of the Catholic Monarchs, of humanistic rhetorical theory.[6]

I would point out that the changes noted by Whinnom also help produce a style conducive to the new, accelerated reading made possible by print, a kind of reading which Marshall McLuhan reminds us greatly fostered reader-identification: "The reader of print...stands in an utterly different relation to the writer from the reader of manuscript. Print gradually made reading aloud pointless, and accelerated the act of reading till the reader could feel 'in the hands of' his author."[7] In other words, the brevity-

Literary History of Spain: The Middle Ages (London: Ernest Benn, 1971), p. 165.

[5] Gilman, *Spain*, p. 326. For numerous seventeenth-century literary references to novels being read aloud in Spain, see Marcos Morínigo, "El teatro como sustituto de la novela en el Siglo de Oro," *Revista de la Universidad de Buenos Aires*, 5th ser., 2 (1957), 41-61. Walter Ong argues that the effects of typography were not fully internalized until the late eighteenth century. See his "Romantic Difference and the Poetics of Technology," Chap. 11 in *Rhetoric*, pp. 255-83, esp. pp. 276-78.

[6] Gili Gaya, pp. xxii-xxiii; Keith Whinnom, "Diego de San Pedro's Stylistic Reform," *Bulletin of Hispanic Studies*, 37 (1960), 1-15.

[7] McLuhan, p. 125. The often-quoted passage from *Cárcel* in which

conscious prose of *Cárcel* is more dense and complex rather than less, and as such is well suited to supplying readers with greater quantities of more detailed information at a faster pace. As Gilman has explained in connection with *Amadís*, another romance that owed its popularity, at least partially, to the printing press: "Reading rapidly and silently (a kind of reading extremely rare before standardization of the page), the new human market was able to absorb reams of grotesque adventures. And the more it read, the better it learned to read.... Not only the form of print on the page (stressed by McLuhan), but also the capacity of straining and ever-multiplying presses to supply (as well as stimulate) the demand for more and more resulted in a brand new kind of reading. In addition to its silence, it was avid, insatiable, self-accelerating...."[8]

Diego de San Pedro was not the only writer of romances to reach the avid new print readers of the 1490's. Indeed, he had a very successful competitor for the flourishing book trade in the person of Juan de Flores. We know virtually nothing about Flores' life, except that he, like San Pedro, published two romances, *Grisel y Mirabella* and *Grimalte y Gradissa*, both believed to have been first printed c. 1495. *Grisel y Mirabella* enjoyed the same remarkable international success as did *Cárcel*, as the existence of its over fifty editions by Cervantes' time attests. *Grimalte y Gradissa*, although apparently not as popular as *Grisel*, is by far the more ambitious of the two works, at least as regards structure.[9] It is *Grimalte* that will concern me in the remaining pages here.

San Pedro abruptly halts a long, detailed description of a judicial duel "por no detenerme en esto que parece cuento de historias viejas" (vol. II of the Whinnom ed. cited in n. 3, p. 117) is interesting in that it combines stylistic *abbreviatio* with an apparent concern for novelty (also expressed by San Pedro in the work's Prologue, p. 80). The author seems intent here on making a generic contrast between the "new," i.e., printed, style of the *novela sentimental*, and the "old" style of the *libros de caballerías*, as yet available only in manuscript form. For a slightly different, but possibly related concern with narrative novelty in Juan de Flores, see below, n. 21. Joseph F. Chorpenning presents a view of *Cárcel* as a fundamentally oral work in "Rhetoric and Feminism in the *Cárcel de Amor*," *Bulletin of Hispanic Studies*, 54 (1977), 1-8.

  [8] Stephen Gilman, "The Novelist and His Readers: Meditations on a Stendhalian Metaphor," in *Interpretation: Theory and Practice*, ed. Charles Singleton (Baltimore: Johns Hopkins University Press, 1969), p. 159.

  [9] Barbara Matulka, *The Novels of Juan de Flores and Their European Diffusion*

What I will comment upon is the series of explicit references to the activities of reading and writing books that Flores weaves through the otherwise standard sentimental plot of *Grimalte*. It has gone generally unremarked that the four principal characters of the work are not only lovers and beloveds, as their literary tradition demands, but that they are also newly conscious of themselves and each other as authors, readers, and characters of books.[10] This type of self-consciousness is unprecedented in Castilian prose fiction, and reinforces on a technical level the stylistic evidence of *Cárcel de Amor* presented above. It suggests that, like his contemporary San Pedro, Juan de Flores incorporated into his second romance[11] an awareness of himself as producer and of his public as excited consumers of an extraordinary new commodity— the printed book.

It will be recalled that *Grimalte y Gradissa*, in addition to narrating the story of the eponymous lovers, continues the tragic tale of

(New York: Institute of French Studies, 1931), pp. xii and 459-75. Only one edition of *Grimalte y Gradissa* has survived. We do have indirect evidence of the work's popularity in the two editions of Maurice Scève's French translation (*La deplourable fin de Flamete*, 1535 and 1536) and in the extensive quotations from *Grimalte* found in *Tristán de Leonís* (1501), as discussed by Pamela Waley ("Juan de Flores y *Tristán de Leonís*," *Hispanófila*, 12 [1961], 1-14).

[10] Flores' romances have received little critical attention, with the notable exception of Pamela Waley's important articles. In one of these ("Fiammetta and Panfilo Continued, "*Italian Studies*, 24 [1969], 15-31), she mentions the repeated references in *Grimalte* to the elegant style of *Fiammetta* and to the fame of its protagonists. Her primary concern, however, here as elsewhere, is to outline the ways in which Flores departs from his model, e.g., by broadening its first-person point of view in order to present the heroine more objectively and to strengthen Pamphilo's characterization. In so doing, she maintains, Flores "moves away from the idealistic portrayal of stock types to observe the behavior of real men and women and to portray them not in isolation or in rare cases but as 'ordinary people.'" My focus here is the extraordinary sensitivity to the relationship between literature and life that Flores bestows on his "ordinary people."

[11] Waley has argued convincingly the precedence of *Grisel y Mirabella* over *Grimalte* and the likelihood that the greater complexity of the latter reflects Flores' newly-acquired familiarity with San Pedro's two romances ("*Cárcel de amor* and *Grisel y Mirabella*: A Question of Priority," *Bulletin of Hispanic Studies*, 50 [1973], 340-56).

Pamphilo and Fiammetta, protagonists of Boccaccio's *L'Elegia di Madonna Fiammetta* (1343-1344). The recreation of the Italian romance in the Spanish one makes *Grimalte* one of the earliest examples of the use of autonomous characters in Spanish literature. Joseph Gillet, in his fundamental survey of the autonomous character in both Spanish and European literature in general, names Flores as a precursor of the kind of authorial detachment so brilliantly exploited by Cervantes in *Don Quijote*. Gillet observes how in *Grimalte* "Boccaccio's characters have stepped out of their novel and outside the control of their author to continue their life in a story by another writer, in fact in another century, and the reader is left with a confusing impression of a timeless world inhabited by age-defying, almost permanent characters." Gillet associates *Grimalte* with such aspects of *Don Quijote* as the priest's mention of his "friend" Cervantes in the *escrutinio de los libros*, and the knowledge members of the ducal court have of Don Quijote and Sancho from having read about them in Part One. In *Grimalte* as in *Don Quijote*, implies Gillet, "fiction overflows its frame into the reality outside and reality may suddenly emerge from fiction."[12]

Neither Gillet nor any of the other scholars who have studied *Grimalte* more detainedly have, however, noted the unusual way in which the structural entanglement of the two love stories, the Castilian and the Italian, is effected, i.e., self-consciously, through the medium of the book. What generates the merging of fiction and reality in *Grimalte* is the presence of its various self-conscious authors, characters, and readers. As we shall see, the act of reading plays an especially important role in *Grimalte*. In the character of Gradissa and her reading of *Fiammetta*, Flores presents a fictionalization of the profound impact of the printed word on the

---

[12] Joseph E. Gillet, "The Autonomous Character in Spanish and European Literature," *Hispanic Review*, 24 (1956), 180-81. For a more theoretical discussion of the use of autonomous characters and the related technique of interior duplication as evidence of "una metafísica relativista constitucionalmente española que se refleja en su arte a través de todo su desarrollo," see Leon Livingstone, "Duplicación interior y el problema de la forma en la novela," in *Teoría de la novela*, ed. Agnes and Germán Gullón (Madrid: Taurus, 1974); the quotation is from p. 164. Walter Ong relates the use of such devices in *Don Quijote* to its being "infinitely more self-consciously involved in typography than any earlier work" (*Interfaces*, p. 291).

responsive reader, of the power of fiction to stimulate such a reader to create new roles or recreate old ones, and of the vital interplay between the worlds of fiction and reality in the reader's imagination. That fictionalization in turn sets in motion a complementary realization, since Gradissa's reading of Boccaccio's work is responsible for bringing its heroine and her fickle lover Pamphilo to life in the book we are reading, about Gradissa and her loyal lover Grimalte.[13]

Flores openly declares his dependence on the Italian work in the introduction to *Grimalte*: "Comiença un breve tractado compuesto por Johan de Flores, el qual por la siguiente obra mudó su nombre en Grimalte, la invención del qual es sobre la Fiometa."[14] Such an affirmation of indebtedness to a written source is, it goes without saying, not at all unusual in medieval letters. Nor is one surprised by Flores' identification of himself with the fictional narrator-protagonist of his romance, an identification made by all of his generic predecessors.

What is unconventional in this introduction is the way Flores exposes, with artful candor, the illusion of reality necessary to the autobiographical form of his romance. By pointing out to the reader that the name Grimalte is merely a pseudonym, Flores

---

[13] It should be noted that the reciprocal techniques of fictionalization and realization form part of the sentimental genre from its inception in Rodríguez del Padrón's *Siervo libre de Amor*. In that romance, as I have shown elsewhere ("'Habla el Auctor': A Reexamination of Boccaccio's *L'Elegia di Madonna Fiammetta* as a Source for the *Siervo libre de Amor*," *Journal of Hispanic Philology*, 4 [1980], 203-36), fiction and reality meet and cross in a mock chain of *auctoritas* created by the narrator-protagonist (the "Auctor") to validate his loyalty in love. He declares himself the "legítimo heredero" of the fourteenth-century poet and already legendary "martyr for love," Macías. Macías, in turn, had been identified previously in the work as the successor in loyalty and fame to the fictional knight Ardanlier, who, as a kind of secular saint of love, is himself a sacrilegious counterpart of a real saint, Santiago de Compostela. Numerous other examples of this technique in the sentimental genre could be adduced; by Flores' time it clearly had become a convention. What is unique to *Grimalte*, I maintain, is the way it explicitly and insistently ties the fictionalization-realization process to the reading and writing of books, and of one book in particular.

[14] *Grimalte y Gradissa*, ed. Pamela Waley (London: Tamesis, 1971), p. 3; accent marks are my addition. All subsequent references to this edition appear as page numbers in the text.

makes explicit what in previous romances of the sentimental genre
was implicit: that very process of fictionalization whereby the "yo"
of the real author becomes the "yo" of a character. We have here
an initial tear in the work's fabric of illusion, a tear that will
gradually widen as the narrative unfolds.[15]

If Flores is initially self-conscious about his role as author, he is
no less sensitive to the role of his readers. After mentioning the
book on which his own is based, the author-narrator provides a
detailed summary of the plot of *Fiammetta* and states its author's
intention "porque algunos de los que esto leyeren por ventura no
habrán visto su famosa scriptura" (p. 3). Flores chooses to respect
the illusion that Fiammetta is the author of her own story. The
reason is clear; such an illusion is necessary to the realization of
Fiammetta in his work.

From the generalized readers of his own autobiography Flores-
Grimalte shifts his focus to one particular and very special reader
of Fiammetta's autobiography: "venida su muy graciosa scriptura a
la noticia de una senyora mía llamada Gradissa, las agenas tristesas
tanto la apassionaron que ella no menos llagada que aquella otra se
sentía" (p. 3). The heroine of *Grimalte* is thus characterized first and
foremost as an exceedingly empathetic reader of sentimental fiction; only secondarily is she presented as the kind of honor-bound
"belle dame sans merci" portrayed by all of her predecessors, from
the "alta señora" of *Siervo libre de Amor* to Laureola in *Cárcel de Amor*.
In fact, compared to Grimalte's vivid descriptions of Gradissa's
emotional involvement with Fiammetta and her sorrow, the hyperbole with which he expresses her cruelty to him seems formu-
laic: "Pues en aquestos comedios que su compassión regnava eran
las fuerças de mis aquexadas requestas, en las quales el meior
tyempo de mi vida fenecía; tanto que yo desto puedo alabarme, que
yo de más constante y ella de más cruel ninguno ygualársenos
pudo" (pp. 3-4). And when Gradissa herself speaks to her lover,
her liberal use of the imagery of courtly love characteristic of all

---

[15] Waley's interpretation of the initial words of *Grimalte* differs from
mine. She states: "Having ignored the creator behind the creation, Flores
in turn conceals himself behind a character of his own novel.... This
preservation of the illusion of reality conforms with Boccaccio's own
narrative form of pseudo-autobiography" (Intro. to *Grimalte*, p. xxix).

sentimental romance often seems less than sincere, and at times even malicious in intent:[16]

> ¿Quién se podrá defender de vuestro continuo seguir? Que si de una parte honestidat me defiende, de la otra vuestras requestas y servicios me vencen, de las quales aquexada no puedo con iusta causa scusarme; mas así como cercada en flaquilla fortalesa menguada de victuallas y toda perterchería, así a partido me viene ser con vos. El qual pues, son notorias a vos las quexas que Fiometa con iusta causa de Pamphilo scrive, y, por cierto, en sus males pensando, quasi como ella las siento, en special que muchas vezes me veo temerosa que si por vuestra mi diesse, yo misma me daría al peligro que ella tiene.   (p. 4)

As these lines illustrate, it is not the courtly code but Gradissa's own impassioned reading of romance that conditions her behavior towards her lover.

In the character of Gradissa, Flores presents a clear case—the earliest in Spanish literature—of *incitación* by means of the written word, to borrow Américo Castro's famous term for the effects of reading *libros de caballerías* on Alonso Quijano. In this sense, the heroine of *Grimalte* should be viewed as the first in a long line of fictive readers in Spanish literature whose lives are transformed by books, the most extreme example being, of course, Alonso Quijano himself. Castro's description of the function of books in the creative process of *Don Quijote* can also be applied to *Grimalte*: "Books appear here, not as coldly objectified realities, with certain ideas or tales to present, but as being read, as a personal experiencing of values in which a person reveals his individuality while incarnating the living substance of the book into his own life.... Books are, therefore, what each reader makes of them by living through them. Literature becomes personalized and individual living reveals its latent poetic dimension...."[17] The personalized literature and poeticized living of *Don Quijote* are, I maintain, the highly evolved descendants of the dual process of realization and fictionalization stimulated by books in *Grimalte*. Through this process

---

[16] Waley, Intro., p. l.

[17] Américo Castro, "Incarnation in *Don Quixote*," in *Cervantes Across the Centuries*, ed. Maír J. Benardete and Angel Flores (New York: Dryden Press, 1947), p. 159.

Flores represents an awareness—not apparent in his earlier work
—of the need for authors and readers to work out credible roles
for themselves for the new medium of print. *Grimalte y Gradissa* is
thus not only about the plight of two interrelated couples; it is also
about the more general problem of "audience readjustment" that
Walter Ong has shown to be a major feature of mature medieval
culture, a culture more focused on reading than any earlier culture
had been.[18]

Gradissa's incitement by *Fiammetta*, like Alonso Quijano's by
Amadís and its congeners, radically alters her own life and the lives
of those around her. Feeling Fiammetta's despair as if it were her
own, Gradissa casts off her inherited, static role as courtly *midons*
and assumes instead the role of one of the compassionate "enamoradas duenyas" to whom Fiammetta expressly addresses her
narration and whose empathy she seeks repeatedly throughout:
"Por la compassión suya con que ella quexa sus danyos a las
enamoradas duenyas, pareçqua que alguna huvo que con piadad
tocó sus oreias, la qual quiero ser yo" (p. 5). Unlike Alonso
Quijano, however, Gradissa realizes and accepts the social cons-
traints that prevent her from personally acting on Fiammetta's
behalf, as the intermediary necessary to reconcile her with Pamphilo: "Y cierto a ello la voluntad me manda que yo vaya en
persona adoquiere que ella esté; pero el fazerlo, sin duda la ver-
guença me lo estorva y lo defiende" (p. 5). Because of this Gradissa
will require the services of a go-between; she finds one in her loyal
suitor, Grimalte.

Gradissa charges Grimalte with a "senyalado servicio," a courtly mission that will decide the outcome of his amorous suit: "es
bueno que se ha de disponer vuestra persona en favor de Fiometa,
y que muestren vuestras obras con ella los desseos que para me
requestar mostrastes. Y si con aquella voluntad havéys seguydo a
mí, que dezíys, con ella trebaiáys en su servicio, soy cierta que
Pamphilo de ser suyo no se defienda" (pp. 4-5). In this way
Grimalte also undergoes a role-change, forced as he is by the
intensity of his beloved's identification with Fiammetta to set aside
temporarily his identity as courtly lover in order to become a
courtly *tercero*. However, Gradissa's challenge is not graciously
accepted by Grimalte, who sees it as an excuse to be rid of him. He

18 Ong, *Interfaces*, pp. 69-81.

is particularly bitter when Gradissa makes the further stipulation that in order to win her favor Grimalte must not only reconcile the Italian lovers, but must also deliver to her a written record of everything that transpires between them "porque yo vea el fin que de la amor reciven aquellos que suyos son" (p. 5).[19] Here again Gradissa affirms the special power and authority of the written word, as Grimalte acquires yet another role—that of *auctor* of a book whose ending holds the key to his future happiness.

Ironically, in view of the initial explicit identification of Grimalte with Juan de Flores, the protagonist complains resentfully of his inadequacy to the role of *auctor*. He compares himself unfavorably to Fiammetta in this respect, revealing that he too has read and admired her famous book: "bien conocéys que la gracia con que Fiometa quexa sus males careçe de mi persona recontaros aquellos .... Que si Dyos de sus gracias parte me diera, yo soy cierto que vos ya fuerays mía, sin haver de hir agora a los stranyos reynos a conqueriros. Mas bien parece que por mengua de no saber quexar mis males ni tractar sigún aquellos que los amores siguen conviene con tal remedio...quedar tal qual yo agora" (p. 7). Grimalte's use of the *topos* of humility in these lines builds upon his earlier reference to Fiammetta as the real author of the book in which she appears as narrator-protagonist. His admiration for her as an *auctor* together with Gradissa's empathy with her as a character set the stage for her subsequent appearance within *Grimalte* itself. At the same time, Grimalte's self-conscious comparison of his writing ability with Fiammetta's draws attention to his own situation as the fictional counterpart of the real author of *Grimalte*.

As for Gradissa, the moment she commissions a sequel to *Fiammetta* from her lover she once more becomes a silent reader of fiction. She does not actively participate in the narrative again until Grimalte delivers the completed "Tractado de Pamphilo y Fiometa" to her, and she reacts to its tragic ending. Nevertheless, her presence as a reader is implicit throughout Grimalte's account. Her interest in the outcome of this particular book is understandable, since her future depends on it as much as Grimalte's or Fiometa's. Clearly, then, if in Grimalte Flores creates an explicit fictionalization of himself, the real author of *Grimalte*, in Gradissa he gives us

---

[19] Waley, "Love and Honour in the *novelas sentimentales* of Diego de San Pedro and Juan de Flores," *Bulletin of Hispanic Studies*, 43 (1966), 267.

an implicit fictionalization of ourselves, the real readers of that same book. Gradissa's reality as reader merges with our own; we are thereby drawn into her illusion that Boccaccio's protagonists are real.

The dual structure of *Grimalte* thus finally resolves itself into that of a book-within-a-book. But the two books stand in a unique relationship to each other, one which enhances the illusion of reality of the whole. Pamphilo and Fiammetta, protagonists of the inner book, are realized by the protagonist of the outer book, Gradissa, or more precisely, by her reading of yet a third book in which Pamphilo and Fiammetta have previously appeared. Simultaneously, Grimalte and Gradissa, protagonists of the outer book, are realized by their intimate involvement in the creation of the inner book, one as its author and the other as its reader. Another layer of interrelatedness is added by the fact that the inner book, the "Tractado de Pamphilo y Fiometa," written by Grimalte, bears a metonymic relationship to the outer book, the *Tractado de Grimalte y Gradissa* written by Juan de Flores, since the two authors are actually one and the same. The point I wish to make is that what makes possible this entire complex structure and the autonomy it grants its characters is the existence of books.

The autonomy of Fiometa and Pamphilo is further heightened as the inner narrative unfolds through the introduction of more readers of *Fiammetta*. Recounting his arduous and as yet unsuccessful search for Fiometa to another traveler he meets at a crossroads, Grimalte explains why he has ceased looking in the towns: "muchas Fiometas en quada villa fallé, porque quien se quería fingir ser ella bien se passava sus tiempos scarnesciéndose de mí" (p. 13). Later, during Grimalte's first interview with Pamphilo, we learn that the latter has inspired a different kind of reaction on the part of male readers: "entre las gentes no hay otro razonar sino de vos. Y ahun los viegos con sperança de resucitar nuevos amores, si algún disfavor reciben de aquélla a quien requestan no crehen que defectos suyos les priven de ser amados, mas antes piensan que vuestras culpas los enbaraçan" (p. 27).

Such comments make us aware that Gradissa's identification with her fictional heroine is not an aberrant or even isolated case. The role-playing of the village girls, the self-delusion of the lustful old men reflect not only the popularity of *Fiammetta* in particular, but also a more generalized openness to the inciting stimulus of books. In this respect also Flores' romance looks ahead, however tentatively, to *Don Quijote*—to Dorotea's playing of the difficult role of Princess Micomicona, or to Don Quijote's attribution of his failures to the enchanters of the *libros de caballerías*. To quote Castro once again: "Each one speaks of the books according to his own experience and impression; and so the book becomes identified with the vital experience of the individual."[20]

Flores' treatment of the incitement generated by the written word generally lacks the ironic tone central to Cervantes' narrative technique. There is, however, at least one clear exception to this rule. It concerns the mysterious fellow-traveler mentioned previously, the "dama de aparado pomposo y honesto [sic] antojos," who Grimalte strongly suspects is the very person he has been seeking. But whereas Grimalte openly shares these suspicions with the reader, with the woman herself he is less direct. When she inquires as to the reason for his difficult journey, he mentions a fateful gift made to his beloved: "pensando hun día cómo meior la serviesse, hun libro llamado Fiometa le levé que leyesse; el qual bien pienso por vos, senyora, ser visto, y podréys haver mirado quántos y quán crueles males quexa de su desconocido Pamphilo a las enamoradas duenyas. Y aquélla por cuyo servicio me moví, contemplando en sus crueles fatiguas, quanto yo por el hun cabo me ayudava, tanto por el otro Fiometa me era enemigua con sus piadozas razones..." (pp. 11-12).[21] This amusing exchange calls to mind the similar conversation in Part Two of *Don Quijote*, in which Sancho and the Duchess discuss Part One: " 'Decidme, hermano escudero: ¿este vuestro señor no es uno de quien anda impresa una historia que se llama *El ingenioso hidalgo Don Quijote de la Mancha*, que tiene por señora de su alma a una tal Dulcinea del Toboso?' 'El mismo es, señora,' respondió Sancho, 'y aquel escudero suyo que

---

[20] Castro, p. 159.

[21] Irony may also be present more generally in Flores' characterization of Grimalte as "a reluctant and unlucky knight" (Waley, "Love," 267-69). Waley makes the interesting suggestion that Flores intentionally uses the courtly relationship of Grimalte and Gradissa as a foil for the very different interaction of the Italian lovers: "as if to point to the reality of the relationship between Pamphilo and Fiometa and the novelty of its representation in fiction, Flores uses the terminology of the old *servicio de amor* between the other pair, and stresses that Pamphilo's behavior is according to *nuevas leyes*" (p. 275).

anda o debe andar en la tal historia...soy yo, si no es que me trocaron en la cuna; quiero decir, que me trocaron en la estampa.'" Fiometa's consciousness of already having been the subject and author of a book when she appears in *Grimalte*, like Sancho and Don Quijote's awareness in Part Two of their appearance in Part One, is the final proof of her "reality."

It is that reality—specifically, Fiometa's despair and death after her rejection by Pamphilo—that Gradissa responds to when Grimalte delivers the completed "Tractado de Pamphilo y Fiometa" to her. She reacts as intensely to the sequel to *Fiammetta* as she did to the original: "Y porque vehays quánto me duele su muerte, devéys sin duda pensar que tan llagada me veo que me haze partir la voluntad de amores, las quales los alegres coraçones piden..." (p. 63). Now, however, Gradissa's intense identification with her literary heroine serves a more traditional reader response, one only hinted at earlier in the book, when Gradissa vowed to take Fiometa as "un spejo de doctrina con que vea lo que con vos [Grimalte] me cumple hazer" (p. 5). Berating her lover for allowing Pamphilo to go unpunished, she concludes: "Así que sin duda, tanto atormentada estoy de las obras de aquell malvado Pamphilo que sin haver mayor vengança de éll no podría conmigo amaros. Porque si ell sin castigo quedasse, ¿quién escarmentaría a vos? Y si agora yo me veo libre, ¿querríades vos que en las redes de aquella Fiometa me lançasse? Por cierto, en quanto pueda, foyré de caher en ellas" (p. 63).

From this point on in the romance, *castigo* and *escarmiento*, the appropriate medieval reader responses to didactic, exemplary works, become the characters' primary motivation. But so fully has Flores realized Boccaccio's fictional characters, that it seems only natural that the *castigo* Pamphilo merits should be fully and voluntarily shared by Grimalte. In the curious epilogue to the principal narrative—an epilogue which also takes the form of a text-within-a-text, being a letter or journal addressed to Gradissa by her lover—the rejected Grimalte joins the repentant Pamphilo in the wilderness, where they live as *hombres salvajes* and share a recurrent vision of Fiometa in torment. The same empathy Gradissa felt for the fictional Fiammetta, Grimalte now demonstrates for the "real" Pamphilo.

Finally, a few words concerning the dates of composition and publication of *Grimalte*. Scholars generally agree with Konrad

Haebler's judgment, based solely on typographical evidence, that both of Flores' romances were printed for the first time *ca.* 1495.[22] The first edition of the Spanish translation of *Fiammetta* (*La Fiometa de Juan Vocacio*) dates from 1496; a second edition that appeared the following year testifies to the immediate success of the first.[23] In the preceding pages I have shown the vital presence of *Fiammetta* in *Grimalte* as a "famosa scriptura," a book that is avidly read, discussed, imitated, and continued. In view of the compelling sense of *Fiammetta's* immediacy as a book in *Grimalte*, it is interesting to speculate that the stimulus for the composition of *Grimalte* was in fact the popularity of the first edition of the Spanish *Fiometa*. We would then be able to give a more precise publication date for the work than its typographical characteristics allow, i.e., a *terminus a quo* of 1496.

One obstacle to this hypothesis is the fact, pointed out by Barbara Matulka, that one of the lyrics inserted in *Grimalte* also appears in the Catalan manuscript *cancionero* entitled *Jardinet d'Orats*. The lyric in question is quoted almost verbatim, and bears the rubric "Phiameta a Grimalte." Since the *Jardinet* was apparently compiled no later than 1486, Matulka concludes that its compiler must have had access to a copy of Flores' work sometime prior to that date. Consequently, she proposes 1480-1485 as the time of *Grimalte's* composition.[24]

22 *Bibliografía ibérica del siglo* XV (The Hague, 1903-1917; rpt. New York: Burt Franklin, 1963), I, 124.

23 The Spanish translation of *Fiammetta* has also come down to us in two fifteenth-century manuscript versions, both preserved in the library of the Escorial (*Bibliography of Old Spanish Texts*, 2nd ed. [Madison: The Hispanic Seminary of Medieval Studies, 1977], nos. 680-82). The 1496 edition of *Fiometa* was unknown to bibliographers until 1926, when it was listed by Leo Olschki in *Le livre illustré au* XVe *siècle* (Florence: Leo Olschki, 1926), p. 27, no. 88. When Boccaccio's work was first translated into Spanish is not known; Farinelli believed it might have been as early as the first decade of the fifteenth century (*Italia e Spagna* [Turin: Fratelli Bocca, 1929], I, 210-11, n. 2).

24 *Novels*, pp. 456-58. A further complication arises when one recalls that the lyric in question, like all those inserted in *Grimalte*, was written not by Flores, but by a collaborator. The authorship of the poetry is acknowledged at the end of the book: "La sepultura de Fiometa, con las coplas y canciones quantas son en este tractado, hizo Alonso de Córdova" (p. 74).

Whether or not the printing of *Fiometa* was the direct stimulus for its recreation and realization in *Grimalte*, thereby reinforcing the symbiosis between the novel and the printing press that has been discovered in Diego de San Pedro's works, does not, I think, invalidate my main point here. To sum up, it is that the narrative technique of *Grimalte*—its self-conscious authors, characters, and readers, its merging of the separate worlds of fiction and reality, and its creation of autonomous characters—reflects creatively the "sudden upheaval in the relationship between literature and society experienced by Rojas and his generation" that was occasioned by the printing press.[25] We can well imagine the surprise and excitement of the fifteenth-century *dama* who, as she eagerly read her newly-printed copy of *Grimalte*, found mirrored in its most unusual protagonists her very excitement.[26]

WASHINGTON, D. C.

[25] Gilman, *Spain*, p. 326.

[26] A shorter version of this essay was read at a meeting of the Division of Spanish Medieval Language and Literature held at the 1981 Modern Language Association Convention. I would like to thank Professor Michael Gerli, of Georgetown University, who heard the earlier version and made valuable suggestions for its revision.

Feliciano de Silva:
A Sixteenth-Century
Reader-Writer of Romance

MARIE CORT DANIELS

READING OR HAVING READ, writing or being in the process of writing, are states and activities which occupy many of the characters who people the pages of *Don Quijote*, states and activities without which some of these characters would not exist. The written word suggests and sustains the life process or serves as the expression of life; it does not fulfill a decorative or illustrative function but appears articulated with the very existence of the individuals involved.[1]

CONTEMPORARY CRITICS FROM Mario Vargas Llosa to Maxime Chevalier have turned their attention to the long-neglected genre of Spanish chivalric fiction. The conventions of the romance are by now well documented. What is missing is a sense of the lives of the readers and of the writers of these books that fed the imaginations of the best and worst minds of sixteenth-century Spain. We need to discern the presence of their authors' personal histories in this fiction. We also need to learn just who read these books and why. Until modern readers are prepared to seek in Don Quijote's library not what we expect to find, but rather what the original readers of such books,

---

[1] Américo Castro, "Incarnation in *Don Quixote*," in *Cervantes Across the Centuries*, ed. Ángel Flores and M. J. Bernadete (New York: Dryden Press, 1947), p. 151.

canon and knight alike, may in fact have found, it will be impossible for us to understand fully the nature of the attraction / repulsion that the romances exert on Cervantes and several generations of sixteenth-century narrators.

We do have, of course, the isolated testimony of famous, self-confessed readers of the romances like Santa Teresa or Juan de Valdés. But aside from the scattered evidence of literary and historical celebrities of the Golden Age, who read these books? The many moral censures of chivalric fiction which continue to appear well into the seventeenth century imply that the majority of readers were highly impressionable young women eager for titillation.[2] Except for the handful of documented readers like Bernal Díaz del Castillo or San Ignacio de Loyola, however, we have little or no evidence of the extent, or social-economic makeup of the public of the first fictional best-sellers in print in Spain. Irving Leonard wonders, for example, why despite the fact that "Circumstantial evidence of the influence of current fiction on the actions of the Conquistador is so considerable... is so little direct testimony available? Why cannot more concrete proof in the form of allusions to fictional works be found in contemporary records?"[3]

If we rely on the usual critical assumptions concerning the readership of the romances, we find the most commonly held belief well summarized by Daniel Eisenberg: "The received opinion concerning the Spanish romances of chivalry during their heyday, the sixteenth century, is that they were works which were read by all classes of society, from the highest to the lowest, but with a considerable predominance of the more numerous lower classes."[4] Such a view is based on a literal acceptance of *Quijote*, I, 50, as an accurate reflection of the classes that would know and read the

---

[2] For a list of the most important attacks against the romances of chivalry, see particularly Marcel Bataillon, *Erasmo y España* (Mexico: Fondo de Cultura Económica, 1966), p. 623; Américo Castro, *El pensamiento de Cervantes* (Barcelona: Noguer, 1972), pp. 60-61; Irving Leonard, *Books of the Brave* (Cambridge: Harvard University Press, 1947), pp. 65-74; Marcelino Menéndez Pelayo, *Orígenes de la novela*, I (Madrid, 1943), pp. 440-66; and F. Sánchez y Escribano, "El sentido cervantino del ataque contra los libros de caballerías," *Anales Cervantinos*, 5 (1955-56), 19-40.

[3] *Books of the Brave*, p. 65.

[4] "Who Read the Romances of Chivalry?" *Kentucky Romance Quarterly*, 20 (1973), 209-33.

romances, but as Eisenberg points out, there is no reason to suspect that when Cervantes referred to the *vulgo* as the common reader of the books of chivalry he was speaking of the lower classes. A careful look at the number of copies of any given edition and the high prices paid for almost all romances of chivalry leads Eisenberg to conclude that in fact the books could be afforded only by wealthy men—if not the nobility to whom they were invariably dedicated, then certainly the more affluent members of the Spanish middle classes.

The standard literary demography of the romances has tended to explain the popularity of the genre by focusing on the second-hand descriptions of the immorality of the works, or by emphasizing the importance of the vicarious sublimation of the heroic impulse in the new generation of leisure class readers created by the end of the Reconquest. Although such explanations may account for a portion of the readership of these fictions, they seem to discount the possibility of any sort of reader identification outside of sex or hero worship.

Stephen Gilman, in his seminal *Spain of Fernando de Rojas,* poses in this regard a question about the nature of the "typical" reader of Spanish romances that suggests a different motivation from those traditionally offered. Gilman finds in Rojas' library certain evidence that the author of *La Celestina* was himself one of the "unlikely addicts" of the romances. The presence among "all the books in romance that I own" of *Amadís de Gaula, Palmerín de Olivia* and *Primaleón*, as well as other lesser known works, leads Gilman to search for an explanation for this "apparent fondness for a genre so alien in its themes and vision from *La Celestina*":

> Precisely because the sense of life expressed by Montalvo and his successors was so unlike Rojas' own, such books offered evasion. Instead of the concentric and concentrated world of *La Celestina*'s strife-ridden city, here (as Cervantes' Canon knew intellectually and his insane interlocutor knew vitally) space and time are open and endless. Adventure replaces domesticity; heroism, haggling; and imagination's elastic horizons, walls and streets.[5]

Within the world of romance *hidalgos,* like Rojas or Alonso Quijano

[5] *The Spain of Fernando de Rojas: The Intellectual and Social Landscape of "La Celestina"* (Princeton: Princeton University Press, 1977), pp. 438-39.

can move without fear of constraint. This is a world where a knight may change his name, not out of fear or prudence, but in confirmation of his own heroic being. Amadís is Amadís whether he calls himself *El Caballero de la Verde Espada* or *El Caballero Griego*. In the same way, movement in the romances is not, to use Gilman's terminology, flight from *desventura* but rather pursuit of *ventura*. These works offer asylum and the pleasures of role-escape to lives of daily anguish.

It seems apparent that if the romances of chivalry offered a possible retreat to their readers, they also must have afforded considerable refuge and consolation to their writers. If Rojas can serve as an example of a serious prose fiction author who sought out the romances as reader, what might we learn by turning to another famous reader and writer of the sixteenth century, Feliciano de Silva? Silva chose to imitate Rojas' *Celestina* as well as the early chivalric fictions, and his background has curious parallels to the life of his master.

In contrast to the majority of the romancers of chivalry, about whom little is known beyond a name, Silva's life is relatively well documented.[6] That he was, despite the calumnies of his critics, modestly well read, is confirmed both by his familiarity with classical themes and by the suggestive entry in his inventory of *bienes*, signed five days before his death, in which he includes "vna arca llena de libros en rromanze y en latin."[7] Such an item seems particularly significant in the context of Silva's other property, largely household goods, and in light of the expensiveness of books. There is every reason to imagine that Silva the reader expended the greater part of his revenue as writer on this vital luxury. Unfortunately the volumes are not itemized, but we can

[6] I am following the chronology suggested by Sydney Cravens in "Feliciano de Silva y los elementos pastoriles en sus libros de caballerías," Diss. University of Kansas, 1972. Cravens' concise summary draws heavily on the following articles: Emilio Cotarelo y Mori, "Nuevas noticias bibliográficas de Feliciano de Silva," *Boletín de la Real Academia Española*, 13 (1926), 129-39; Erasmo Buceta, "Algunas noticias referentes a la familia de Feliciano de Silva," *Revista de Filología Española*, 18 (1931), 390-92; Narciso Alonso Cortés, "Feliciano de Silva," *Boletín de la Real Academia Española*, 20 (1933), 382-404; Constance Rose, *Alonso Núñez de Reinoso: The Lament of a Sixteenth-Century Exile*, (Rutherford: Farleigh Dickinson University Press, 1971).

[7] Alonso Cortés, "Feliciano de Silva," p. 396.

assume that his collection would include both *La Celestina* and the greater part of the *Amadís* family. It would also be natural to suspect that his library coincided in many cases with that of Fernando de Rojas.

Feliciano, son of Tristán de Silva, was born around 1491. Educated, like Rojas, at Salamanca, Silva spent almost his entire life in Ciudad Rodrigo where the Silvas had long been one of the leading families. Although he earned extraordinary fame in his lifetime, Feliciano de Silva appears to have led a life of almost total isolation from the world outside his *patria chica*. One obvious explanation of this quiet *vida apartada* of the Regidor of Ciudad Rodrigo, long suspected by critics, is the questionable *limpieza* of his family.[8] Feliciano's *converso* status has yet to be confirmed, but there is very strong circumstantial evidence. The very title of *regidor* is sufficient information to begin to alert our suspicions, and Silva's closest friends are among the most prominent *converso* authors of his generation, Jorge de Montemayor and Núñez de Reinoso. But even if we suspend judgment concerning Silva's own background, there can be no doubt about the undesirable blood of his wife, Gracia Fe, whom he married in 1520. The marriage enraged Silva's relatives and caused serious problems for the descendants of the couple. Gracia's *converso* stain ultimately prevented the entrance of her grandson, Don Fernando de Toledo y Silva, into the order of Santiago in 1596.[9]

Silva's marriage, with its very real threat to the *opinión* of the entire family, finds fascinating expression in his own romances. As early as 1926 Cotarelo had suggested, half whimsically, that Silva "quiso ser novelista de su propia y real existencia" by circulating fictional genealogies of his wife, attributing her birth to the indiscretions first of the Duke of Arcos, and finally to Don Diego de Mendoza, to whom he dedicated *Amadís de Grecia*.[10] At the conclusion of Book One of the work Silva includes a fictional representation of his difficult courtship of Gracia Fe in the famous *Sueño de Feliciano de Silva*.[11] The *Sueño* bears a remarkable resemblance to the

---

8 Cravens, p. 22.

9 See Cotarelo, "Nuevas noticias bibliográficas," pp. 132-39.

10 Cotarelo, p. 139.

11 The *Sueño de Feliciano de Silva* has been published separately with commentary by Henry Thomas in *Dos romances anónimos del siglo XVI* (Madrid: Fontanet, 1917). All citations from the *Sueño* come from this text.

story of Felesindos, the knight whose amorous sufferings are related in the second half of Reinoso's *Historia de los amores de Clareo y Florisea* (1552). Constance Rose, in her illuminating study of the life and work of Reinoso, suggests that Felesindos is in fact "a portrait of Núñez de Reinoso's Spanish friend Feliciano de Silva, whose adventures the narrator (Isea-Reinoso) observed and recorded in a manner evocative of Silva's own literary style."[12]

Although the allegory of the *Sueño* itself is of considerable interest, and betrays the influence of the sentimental romance on Silva's early writings, by far the most interesting aspect of the work for our purposes is the way in which Silva is able to convert the anguish of his personal situation into a conventionalized literary experience. After a series of confrontations with allegorical personifications like Pensamiento, Dolor, Tormento, Conocimiento, and others, Silva is guided by Desesperación to the Castle of Love, "tan torreado y tan hermoso, que yo pense ser el parayso terrenal, tal estava" (*Sueño*, p. 66). Juan Rodríguez del Padrón detaches himself from the swarm of Love's attendants to greet Silva and personally guide the lover to the very throne of Cupid himself. But before Silva can climb the dais, Love's secretary reads aloud the Twelve Commandments of Love.

Henry Thomas points out that these *mandamientos* were suppressed in the Lisbon edition (1589) of *Amadís de Grecia* because of their sacrilegious nature. Although the majority merely repeat the conventional laws of courtly love (as in law 12, "que solo su coraçon sea testigo de su secreto," p. 68), the first is far too dangerous to avoid censure in the late sixteenth century: "El primero mandamiento de nuestro Dios de Amor es, que su magestad sea temido, amado y acatado sobre todas las cosas" (p. 67). In an ironic parody of Inquisitional procedures Silva goes on to *confess* publicly his orthodoxy, swearing to the Tribunal that he has obeyed all the commandments and committed no *knowing* heresy against love:

> yo, como en mi no viesse aver *errado* contra ninguno de aquellos mandamientos; *jure en la fe* de mi señora a aver los guardado. Para en *prueva y testimonio de mi limpieza* presente aquellos gozos y excelencias de mi pensamiento, con todas las *obras* mias; las quales *vistas* y *examinadas* ser sin *heregia* ni *yerro* contra los doze

---

[12] *Alonso Núñez de Reinoso: The Lament of a Sixteenth-Century Exile*, p. 33.

mandamientos, el Dios de Amor dio una gran boz, diziendo 'Este es mi hijo muy amado, con el qual yo mucho me he gozado.' (p. 68)

Despite the lighthearted tone of the passage, and the entire allegory's obvious debt to the sentimental romance tradition, the language is simply too charged with meaning to be dismissed as playful banter, in light of the serious difficulties Silva and his family faced as a result of his imprudent marriage.

In many of his romances Silva adopts an unusually tolerant attitude towards the religious convictions of his pagan heroes, which is in marked contrast to the treatment of non-Christians by other chivalric authors, particularly Montalvo, who spares no sympathy for the enemies of the True Faith. Although biographical speculation can prove as unrewarding as it is dangerous in an author as little known as Silva, still there is considerable evidence to suggest that his personal suffering as a result of the intolerance shown his own wife because of her *converso* status may have led him to express a far more than literary interest in the question of the conversion of his heroes.

Amadís de Grecia, for example, lives for the greater part of his *History* as a pagan, unaware that he is the son of Lisuarte and Onoloria, Christians both. When his squire, a Christian renegade, prudently advises Amadís to defer his plans for the reconquest of Persia in the name of paganism until he is sure that his parents are not Christians, Amadís affirms the personal freedom of the individual to accept the faith that reason, rather than mere custom or birth, might decree: "si mis padres fueron Christianos, o que no lo sean, *en mi mano es tener la ley que mejor fuere*, que por esso tiene el hombre diferencia entre las bestias con la razon que los dioses en el pusieron, pues para escoger lo bueno, y dexar lo no tal tiene libre albedrio..." (*Amadís de Grecia*, 9, f. 10).[13]

Silva makes it clear that despite his pagan beliefs, Amadís is the moral equal or even superior to the Christians that he encounters.

---

[13] Quotations, indicating book, chapter and folio number, come from the following editions of Silva's romances: *Amadís de Grecia* (Sevilla: Cromberger, 1542); *Florisel de Niquea* I and II (Zaragoza: Domingo de Portonariis Ursino, 1584); *Florisel de Niquea* IV (Salamanca: Andreas de Portonariis Ursino, 1551).

Badly wounded, and in the territory of enemies, Amadís asks an old man for directions to a nearby castle to be cured:

> Si vos fuessedes Christiano como yo, dixo el viejo, yo os diria lo que pedis. Amigo, dixo el, aunque no lo sea lo deveis de hazer, porque la virtud no se pierde do quier que se haga, pues haziendose no puede dexar de ser virtud, ansi que si en vos la ay dezidme lo que os pregunto, pues haziendo la en vos queda y no comigo, y pues soys mas obligado a vos que a nayde, no dexeis de hazer bien pudiendo lo hazer, que los dioses no son estimados si no por el bien que dellos se espera, y en ellos ay, *assi que aunque no seays de su ley, no dexais de semejardes en lo bueno, que otro tanto hare yo de lo que bien me pareciere de vuestro Dios, aunque soy pagano*... (9, f. 10)

Although the young Amadís de Grecia is just as pious and sententious as Montalvo's zealous crusader Esplandián, nowhere does Silva demonstrate the intense hatred for non-Christians displayed in *Las sergas,* written while the expulsion of the Jews from Spain is still a recent memory. Montalvo praises the Catholic Monarchs who "no cansando con sus personas, no retiniendo sus tesoros, echaron del otro cabo de las mares aquellos infieles que tantos años el reino de Granada tomado y usurpado, contra toda ley y justicia tuvieron. Y... *limpiaron de aquella sucia lepra, de aquella malvada herejia* que en sus reinos sembrada por muchos años estaba, así de los visibles como de los invisibles..." (*BAE*, 40, *102*, p. 505).

Even when Amadís de Grecia discovers that he is the lost heir to the Greek Empire (Chapter 62), he resists conversion and refuses to be baptized as his father Lisuarte and the rest of the Greek princes urge. When he finally does become a Christian (Chapter 92), it is not to satisfy his family but because he discovers directly the First Cause in the famous Torre del Universo constructed by the magicians Urganda, Alquife, and Zirfea:

> ...subio a lo alto della [la torre], que como encima fue, luego el mundo y los cielos le fue representado, y sus movimientos...y miro en lo alto de todos los cielos y vio el carro triunfal en que el solo soberano Señor estava, *luego le vino conoscimiento claro del engaño* que hasta alli avia tenido y hincando los ynojos en tierra lo adoro, renegando de los dioses que hasta alli avia tenido, prometiendo en servicios de los enmendar... (92, f. 192)

Once Amadís, disguised as the Amazon maiden Nereyda, finally seduces Niquea, he converts her also with "las muchas y buenas

razones que a su amiga le supo dezir." Thus religious conviction is
not the product of dogma or conquest but of reflection and insight.
Silva's attitude is made even clearer in *Florisel de Niquea*, Part IV.
Rogel de Grecia converts his companion and former rival Gran-
dabadel, king of Sufiana. Fired with the zeal of his new faith, the
giant impatiently inquires why Christians do not force the pagans
to recognize the superiority of their *ley de Cristo*:

> No se porque los principes christianos no hazen por fuerça
> guardar su ley, a los que por virtud no la admiten. En lo que esta
> en ley natural, dixo el principe, teneys razon: pues no pueden los
> hombres naturalmente negar tal obligacion en las leyes de bien
> ordenada republica, que de la ley Evangelica salen: *mas lo que della
> esta en la fe*, como cosa sobrenatural, sobre toda razon humana, *no
> es licito por fuerça hazer creer sus misterios....* Assi que *quanto a la parte
> moral*, pareceme a mi que es justo los Principes Christianos,
> hazer a los infieles guardar la ley Evangelica, como ministros del
> derecho natural de Christo por el poder que del tienen. *Mas lo
> que toca la fe como voluntariamente se a de recebir, y la voluntad de ninguna
> fuerça pueda ser constreñida, no se a de procurar con la fuerça*, hasta ser
> admitido lo que no basta para ello ninguna fuerça, si la voluntad
> libremente no recibe la fe que esta sobre toda razon. (*85*, f. 145)

What saves this speech from simple moral commonplace is the
implied criticism of contemporary Christian, and particularly Spanish, attitudes toward faith and conversion. Rogel criticizes Christians because they mistakenly attempt to convert by force, rather
than by example and sacrifice. Christ, he points out, chose to
sacrifice Himself instead of those sinners who did not believe in
Him. He urged that his followers "sojuzgassen el mundo al reves
delos principios humanos, *muriendo y no matando*" (f. 145).

There seems little doubt that this passage is an indirect indictment of the harshness of the Inquisition, which attempted not
only to enforce external religious and moral practices but to
monitor individual conviction as well. Silva's own religious orthodoxy is not in question here. There is no reason to suspect that he
was anything other than a pious and conventionally devout Christian. Indeed, what he seems to be advocating is a program of
religious instruction in preparation for conversion not unlike that
championed by Hernando de Talavera a generation before, in
which persuasion and reason prevail over terror.

In addition to this tendency towards religious tolerance, Silva emphasizes the subordination of lineage to virtue, an attitude that is in keeping with the peculiar circumstances of his own marital situation. If he chose to describe allegorically his courtship of Gracia Fe in the *Sueño*, another plot incident of *Amadís de Grecia* reflects with equal vividness Silva's compassionate view of the problems of marriages between unequal *estados*. This compassion is tempered, as in Cervantes, by the conventional reliance on the adage "blood will out," but Silva is careful to have his apparently plebeian heroine secure a promise of marriage before the truth of her noble birth is revealed.

The episode is the well-known story of the shepherdess Silvia, long-lost daughter of Lisuarte, and sister of Amadís de Grecia. Brought up by peasants, Silvia becomes a *pastora* but feels an innate superiority that compels her to reject the suit of her fellow shepherd Darinel as unworthy. Florisel de Niquea, disguised as a shepherd, proves a more formidable suitor, but Silvia withstands his assaults with virtue intact. Neither Florisel nor Silvia is aware of their true relationship: Florisel, Amadís de Grecia's son, is Silvia's nephew. In spite of her apparent low birth, Silvia feels a justifiable haughtiness when Florisel laments that love does not recognize reason, since it has permitted him to lower his thoughts and "la obligacion de la sucession de mi alta sangre a ajuntalle por matrimonio con una pastora no solo perdiendo reynos, y señorios que con otra mi ygual esperava, mas *abaxando la mi real sangre que con tantos trabajos y limpieza de la honra de mis abuelos y padres me fue otorgada*" (*Florisel*, I, 20, f. 38).

In a spirited rebuttal Silvia ably employs Aristotelian logic to defend her worthiness to be loved despite the differences in worldly estate:

> todo quanto dezis quiero consentir, sino solo en dezir que no avia razon para me amar por la diferencia de los estados. Y a esto respondo que mas ventaja tiene la causa principal en perfeccion que lo que della sucede; quien puso linaje y estado en los hombres sino los merecimientos de los que por ellos se señalaron en personas donde con antiguedad aquella nobleza acompañada de riqueza con que dieron a sus decendientes claridad? *Pues luego que defecto en mi persona puede la vuestra grandeza poner si por persona se adquirieron los reales estados... que mi señor, si en mi flaqueza de virtud y limpieza y honestidad con falta de hermosura se conosciera, razon tuvierades para dezir, que os abaxastes por mi, mas pues en esto yo a ninguna princesa conozco ventaja, no os la quiero consentir.* (f. 38)

In contrast to the social significance of *limpieza* as Don Florisel has used the word, which in this context can only refer to purity of blood, Silvia opposes her sense of integrity and, specifically here, her chastity. She proves her moral superiority when separated from Florisel by a shipwreck, and threatened with rape by a gang of thieves. Rather than submit, Silvia determines to kill herself, appropriately with Don Florisel's sword, "como aquella que su naturaleza real la obligava a lo que su habito encubria" (*Florisel* I, 20, f. 39). If Silva justifies Silvia's extraordinary beauty and elevated sense of moral purpose as an inevitable result of her noble parentage, he at the same time insists on her personal conception of honor as her only inheritance.

Silvia is unwilling to accept less than total homage from Anastarax when she rescues him from the enchantment in which he has been captive for more than fifteen years, "siendo el tan alto principe, y ella tan baxa donzella, que el mayor bien que tiene[s] es guardar ganado" (25, f. 46). She refuses to become his mistress when he balks at marrying one of such lowly descent: "mucho le peso en saber que era de baxo nascimiento: porque no podia pensar con que satisfazer al amor que le tenia, ni el cargo en que le era sino casando conella: el qual [Anastarax]...se llego a Silvia... provando si podia ganarle la voluntad sin obligarse a casamiento" (25, f. 46). It is only after Anastarax publicly betrothes Silvia, accepting her on human values alone regardless of her lineage, that the true facts of her birth are made known. Although this theme is certainly a commonplace in the literature of the period, Silva devotes an extraordinary number of speeches to the defense of Silvia (possibly an anagram for the Silva family?),[14] and this assertion of purely personal values apart from social definition does seem to reflect attitudes shaped by Feliciano de Silva's own history.

Castro, Gilman, Bataillon, Rose and others have demonstrated the degree to which a set of literary conventions can incarnate the agonizing circumstances of sixteenth-century experience and consciousness. Surely it is not accidental that the three master escape artists of the first half of the century should have been both

---

[14] Sydney Cravens (p. 66) also suspects that Silvia may represent Silva, but he does not discuss the possible biographical significance of such an anagram.

friends and fellow travelers. Montemayor, Núñez de Reinoso and Silva, as fashioners of the most popular romances of their day, are united in their conscious literary efforts to distance themselves from the everyday anguish of their lives through the retreat into the comforting bosom of romance. Yet within that literary shelter, as we have argued in this brief examination of the presence of Silva's own personal history within his romances, there lay dormant the promise of counter-attack and the promise of a more tolerant, less constricted world view—even the hope of *convivencia.* If ultimately Cervantes proved the only author of his age to integrate completely the threatening outer world of desperately particular time and space with the poetic truth of romance within one single narrative frame, we should not underestimate for that reason the importance of the previous experiments of men like Feliciano de Silva in the pastoral, byzantine, and chivalric romances which helped to create and nourish this unique process of incarnation.

COLORADO COLLEGE

Alonso Núñez de Reinoso's Contribution to the Creation of the Novel

CONSTANCE HUBBARD ROSE

URING THE SACK OF Buda in 1526, the manu-
script of Heliodorus' *Aethiopica* was discovered
in "Corvina," the library of King Matthias
Corvinus of Hungary. This third-century
romance was almost immediately translated
from the original Greek into Latin and from
Latin into various European languages; its
popularity, in turn, led to the translation of
Clitophon and Leucippe by Heliodorus' lesser-known contemporary
Achilles Tatius. The vogue, in Renaissance Europe, for the Byzantine romance can be attributed to a number of factors: it res-
ponded to humanistic interest in the revival of classical learning,
provided an exercise in literary suspense with its complex, sinuous
plots, and supplied new material to the expanded reading public
created by the printing press. Moreover, it recreated an adven-
turous atmosphere corresponding to the excitement generated by
the voyages of discovery and satisfied the demand for knowledge
of faraway places or of ancient times in a world of newly-dis-
covered temporal and geographical relationships. The story might
have ended there, with a series of translations, had it not been for
an all but unknown Spaniard, Alonso Núñez de Reinoso, who saw
the possibility of adapting Tatius' tale to his own particular use—

that of fashioning a fictional surrogate self.[1] The rest is literary history.

The work which he created, *Historia de los amores de Clareo y Florisea y de los trabajos de la sin ventura Isea* (Venice, 1552), is only partially based on Tatius' work; strictly speaking, it is a compendium of the fictional forms available in Reinoso's day—half Byzantine, half chivalric, set in a pastoral frame.[2] It also differs from its source in tone and intent. Whereas *Clitophon and Leucippe* is a young work, energetic and exciting, at times lewd, at times humorous, Reinoso's romance is bathed in an autumnal light and is related in a stately cadence, and it is sad, immensely sad. Those critics who persist in calling Reinoso the father of the Byzantine romance in Spain, unintentionally do him a disservice, for this is to suggest a false dependency on Tatius' work and to deny him his role as an innovator, as a creator of fictions. Yet, by examining the Byzantine component of *Clareo y Florisea*, it is possible to appreciate the originality of Alonso Núñez de Reinoso's contribution to the creation of the novel which would come to fruition with Miguel de Cervantes.[3]

A self-conscious artist who was quite aware of what he was doing and who wanted to share his professional secrets with the

---

[1] In *Alonso Núñez de Reinoso: The Lament of a Sixteenth-Century Exile* (Rutherford: Fairleigh Dickinson University Press, 1971), I discuss the vogue for the Byzantine romance, pp. 157-62. For more information, consult: Heliodorus of Emesa, *An Ethiopian Romance*, intro. and trans. Moses Hadas (Ann Arbor: University of Michigan, 1957); *Historia etiópica de los amores de Teágenes y Cariclea* (trans. Fernando de Mena, 1587), ed. Francisco López Estrada (Madrid: Real Academia Española, 1954); Marcel Bataillon, *Erasmo y España*, trans. Antonio Alatorre (México: Fondo de Cultura, 1966), pp. 438-70; E. C. Riley, *Cervantes's Theory of the Novel* (Oxford: Clarendon Press, 1962); Alban K. Forcione, *Cervantes, Aristotle and the "Persiles"* (Princeton: Princeton University Press, 1970); and Ben Edwin Perry, *The Ancient Romances: A Literary Account of their Origins* (Berkeley: University of California, 1967).

[2] In addition to the three stated here, Antonio Prieto in *Morfología de la novela* (Barcelona: Planeta, 1975) lists a fourth fictional form, the sentimental romance, which he finds structurally present in the narrative voice—an intriguing interpretation.

[3] In this specific instance, I use the word "novel" to mean the modern novel. Although Riley, *Cervantes's Theory of the Novel*, also uses the term in relation to pre-Cervantine prose fiction, Forcione, *Cervantes*, insists on "romance" as the proper designation for such early works. Perry, how-

reader, Reinoso confesses that while browsing in a Venetian book-store, he came across a work called the *Amorosi ragionamenti* and, attracted by the title, decided to read further. The book, he soon realized, was an incomplete Italian version, via Latin, of the Greek original. While he does not reveal all the details, it is clear that the volume which inspired him and which transformed this deracinated Spaniard from poet to novelist was Lodovico Dolce's translation of Tatius' *Clitophon and Leucippe.*[4] Reinoso further informs us that his work is in no sense a translation ("[estoy] imitando y no romançando"), but that he made use of the plot ("no uso más que de la invención y algunas palabras") as a means for transmitting events in his own life and in those of his friends. "Debaxo de su invención ay grandes secretos," he cautions.[5]

ever, in *The Ancient Romances,* while preferring the term "romance," uses it interchangeably with "early novel." In itself, *Clareo y Florisea* causes considerable generic confusion, for while its surface is fantasy, its core is real. After considerable thought, I have chosen, for the present study, to refer to Reinoso's narrative as a romance, as suggested by Dorothy Severin, in order to distinguish prose from poetry of the same modal concern. Nevertheless, I do find the expression "Greek Romance" somewhat misleading for chronological and geographical reasons, and favor the alternative "Byzantine." An appropriate term for the wandering protagonist in this and other works dealing with exile, is, as I suggested in *Alonso Núñez de Reinoso,* "peregrino." Indeed, López Estrada has rechristened the "novelas bizantinas de aventuras" of Menéndez Pelayo (*Orígenes de la novela*) as "libros de aventuras peregrinas" in his *Siglos de Oro: Renacimiento* (Barcelona: Editorial Crítica, 1981), p. 276.

4 *Amorosi ragionamenti. Dialogo nel quale si racconta un compassionevole amore di due amanti,* tradotto per m. Lodovico Dolce, dal fragmento d'uno antico Scrittor Greco...(Venice: Gabriel Giolito de Ferraris, 1546). Dolce's translation was based on *Narrationis amatoriae fragmentum e graeco in latinum conversum,* Annibale Cruceio interprete (Lyons: S. Gryphium, 1544). Copies of these works can be found in the Harvard College Library and in the Biblioteca Marciana of Venice. The good fortune which led Reinoso to the *Amorosi ragionamenti* also supplied him with an editor (Dolce) and a publisher (Giolito), who had already issued an Italian translation of Heliodorus' romance. A later adaptation of Tatius' work, Diego de Agreda y Varga's *Los más fieles amantes* (Madrid: Juan de la Cuesta, 1617), was written without reference to Reinoso's book.

5 These remarks are contained in two letters written from Venice in 1552 and addressed to his patron, Juan Micas (Joseph Nasi), in Venice, and to Juan Hurtado de Mendoza, Señor de Torote, in Madrid. The epistles preface the two separate sections of Reinoso's work, whose full title is *La historia de los amores de Clareo y Florisea y de las tristezas y trabajos de la sin ventura*

Because his life was the substance of his art, to understand his work, it is necessary to examine his life; yet, paradoxically, in order to reconstruct the outline of his life, it is imperative to consult his work.[6] From what can be gleaned from his romance, together with its prefatory letters and appended poems, and from a handful of hard-sought facts which deal primarily with the lives of his acquaintances, it can safely be assumed that Alonso Núñez de Reinoso was born at the end of the fifteenth century into an upper middle-class *converso* family associated with the powerful Mendozas of Guadalajara. To please his parents, Alonso studied law—"Padezco gran dolor y sufro males / en leyes estudiar" (No. 16), he complained. The profession held little interest for him, preferring as he did *belles lettres* to "letras de ganar" (No. 13).[7] At the university, however, he met Feliciano de Silva who, despite what Diego Hurtado de Mendoza had to say, seems to have strayed out of

Isea, natural de Epheso, Con otras obras en verso, parte al estilo Español, y parte al Italiano, agora nuevamente sacada a luz. The quotations appear at I, pp. 2 and 3, and II, p. 4, respectively. Copies can be found in the Biblioteca Nacional, Biblioteca Marciana, and the Hispanic Society of America.

6 In *Alonso Núñez de Reinoso,* I devote forty pages (pp. 21-60) to his biography, and some of the ninety-two footnotes refer to previously unedited material. Useful studies are Bataillon's pioneer work, "Alonso Núñez de Reinoso et les marranes portugais en Italie," *Revista da Faculdade de Letras de Lisboa,* 3 ser., 1 (1957: *Miscelánea de estudos em honra do Prof. Hernâni Cidade*), 1-21; those of Carolina Michaëlis de Vasconcelos, *Novos estudos sobre Sá de Miranda* (Lisboa: Imprensa Nacional, 1911), *Poesias de Francisco Sá de Miranda* (Halle: M. Niemeyer, 1885), and Bernardim Ribeiro e Cristóvão Falcão, *Obras* (Coimbra: Imprensa Universidade, 1923); Eugenio Asensio's "Alonso Núñez de Reinoso, 'gitano peregrino' y su égloga 'Baltea,' *Studia Hispánica in Honorem R. Lapesa,* I (Madrid: Gredos, 1972), 119-37; Helder Macedo's *Do significado oculto da "Menina e Moça"* (Lisboa: Moraes Editores, 1977); my "New Information on the Life of Joseph Nasi, Duke of Naxos: The Venetian Phase," *Jewish Quarterly Review,* 60 (1970), 334-44, and "Spanish Renaissance Translators. I. The Exile and the Diplomat; II. Alfonso de Ulloa, Ariosto, and the Word *Marrano,*" *Revue de Littérature Comparée,* 45 (1971), 554-72.

7 (15) "Alonso Nunnez de Reynoso al Sennor Feliciano de Silva," and (13) "Síguese un romance," whose lines are expanded upon in (14) "Comienza la glosa deste romance," quoted from the appendix to *Alonso Núñez de Reinoso.* In the introduction, I describe the poems and assign them numbers. This is the first time, save for two poems included in Durán's *Romancero,* BAE, 16 (Madrid: Rivadeneyra, 1851), that Reinoso's poetry has been made accessible to the reader subsequent to its 1552 publication.

Ciudad Rodrigo on more than one occasion, at least as far as
Salamanca and perhaps even into Portugal.[8] The established
author and the aspiring poet became fast friends, and young
Alonso was treated as one of the family. Certainly Silva introduced
him, by letter or in person, to a group of Portuguese poets headed
by Francisco Sá de Miranda and Bernardim Ribeiro, with whom he
established a deep friendship. When Reinoso was obliged to flee
Spain, he joined his Portuguese friends on the country estate of
the Pereira brothers in Cabaceiros do Basto. In the poetry of this
literary academy, Reinoso is consistently portrayed as an embit-
tered exile, bereft of family, friends and fortune.[9]

In Portugal, it must have seemed as if fortune smiled on him,
though briefly, for in addition to the literary circle in which he
participated, he became acquainted with the most famous Portuguese Jewish banking family of the century, that of Gracia Mendes
(Beatriz de Luna) and her nephew Joseph Nasi (João Miques or
Juan Micas), the future advisor to Selim, the son of Suleiman the
Magnificent. Dona Gracia extended to the exiled poet the aid she
offered to other refugees from the Inquisition, "peregrina gente /

[8] "Veis ahí a Feliciano de Silva, que en toda su vida salió más lejos que
de Ciudad Rodrigo a Valladolid, criado siempre entre Nereydas y Dara-
ydas, metido en la torre del Universo, a donde estuvo encantado...diez y
ocho años," *Carta del Bachiller de Arcadia*, in *Sales españolas o Agudezas del ingenio
nacional*, I, ed. Antonio Paz y Melia (Madrid: Escritores Castellanos, 1890),
p. 80. Silva, author of four books in the *Amadís* series, is the object of
Reinoso's literary homage as Felesindos, "el caballero de las Esperas du-
dosas," in the chivalric adventures which constitute the second portion of
Clareo y Florisea. For a refreshingly positive opinion of Silva's work, see
Daniel Eisenberg, *Romances of Chivalry in the Spanish Golden Age* (Newark,
Delaware: Juan de la Cuesta, 1982), pp. 75-85.

[9] In my 1971 book, I based my theory about the contact between
Reinoso, Sá de Miranda, Ribeiro, Silva and others on internal evidence,
that is, from the poetry of the Basto academy where the first three
addressed each other by their pastoral pseudonyms, dealt with identical
topics, reworked the same material, and even borrowed lines from each
other. See especially the section called "Portrait and Self-Portrait," pp. 69-
84. In his 1972 article, "Alonso Núñez de Reinoso, 'peregrino gitano,'"
Asensio, who supplied documentary evidence which supports my hypothesis, argued that the poet was an early Romantic who enjoyed suffering
for his art. It is to be hoped that Asensio, who has tantalized us with a
description of the manuscript, will one day make public the eclogue in his
possession.

de ella siempre recibió" (No. 1), no matter the country in which she found herself. Reinoso became attached to this wandering household as a tutor. When, with the establishment of the Portuguese Inquisition in 1536, it became necessary to move on, after one abortive attempt to leave the country, he followed his protectors, first to Antwerp in 1545[10] and later to Venice and Ferrara. In Italy, among their many commercial and cultural activities, Juan Micas and his aunt sponsored the printing of Reinoso's book and those of his friends, the Portuguese Bernardim Ribeiro and the Italian Hortensio Lando.[11] After the publication of his book, further trace of Núñez de Reinoso is lost completely. Perhaps he was one of the forty horsemen who comprised the splendid retinue of Gracia Mendes on her triumphant entrance into Constantinople in 1553, perhaps not. The date and place of his death, like those of birth, are unknown. The only uncontestable date in the life of this peripatetic poet is 1552, the year of the publication of his *Clareo y Florisea*, a book composed out of his travels and travails.

That Alonso Núñez de Reinoso considered the facts of his own life a suitable subject for publication is in itself unusual. He was not, after all, famous like Cellini. There was little in European literary tradition before Reinoso to suggest that the life of a minor poet held any interest. To be sure, the anthropocentric world view of the Renaissance opened up the possibility and two Italian masters served him as models. While Boccaccio's *Fiammetta* remains a literary landmark as an account of a fictive life, it recounts the life of another, despite its author's peripheral presence.[12] Petrarch,

---

[10] The fact that Ribeiro's "Ao longo de hua ribeira," was printed, probably posthumously, in Antwerp in 1545 suggests Reinoso's presence in Flanders where Juan Micas resided until 1546. The poem is but one of two published before the printing of the Portuguese writer's book, *Menina e moça*, in Ferrara in 1554, for which the Spaniard and his patron were also presumably responsible.

[11] For those interested in the Mendes-Nasi family, see my "New Information" for bibliographical references. I initially was able to identify Núñez de Reinoso's benefactor through a passage in *Viaje de Turquía*, attributed to Cristóbal de Villalón in the edition of Manuel Serrano y Sanz, *Autobiografías y memorias*, NBAE, 2 (Madrid: Bailly-Baillière, 1905), p. 131a-b.

[12] Despite Prieto's statement, "... intencionadamente, quiebro una sucesión cronológica en la trayectoria de la narrativa sentimental europea

with the intimacy of his *Secretum*, is surely the precursor of the secular self-revelatory genre, factual or fictional.[13] Of the first-person narratives created in the Iberian Peninsula in the 1550's, only Reinoso's work stands out as truly related to its author's life.[14] Lázaro, for example, could never have written his own tale as it stands, nor could his anonymous author, for reasons of education, ironic distance, and deprecatory attitude, be associated with his anti-hero. But in Reinoso's literary confession, the central figure does speak for its author.

Isea, his heroine-narrator, has retreated to the Isla Pastoril where she hopes to find solace by recording the sad events of her life.[15] Hers is a retrospective recounting of the events which have led to her present hopeless plight, a literary confession in which she examines and imparts her subjective response to adversity. In addition to release from her sorrows, Isea hopes, through her

para no caer en el tópico de hacer descender la sentimental española de la *Fiammetta...* de Boccaccio," p. 242, there is no doubt of the influence of Boccaccio's book on Reinoso, either directly (and he read Italian) or through Ribeiro. See *Alonso Núñez de Reinoso*, pp. 129-35. In *Fiammetta*, Boccaccio is present as an image reflected in the eye of the female narrator, a technique later used by Lope in the poem, "Pechos sobre una torre."

13 Saint Augustine, in his *Confessions*, may be considered the father of the nonsecular or sacred autobiography.

14 Without entering into the problems of authorship, one can safely assume that Pedro de Urdemalas of the dialogued novel or fictive travelog, *Viaje de Turquía*, which owes much to the Byzantine romance, in some respects speaks for his creator. Andrés Laguna, or whoever the author may be (see the edition of Fernando García Salinero [Madrid: Cátedra, 1980] for a discussion of the problem and for a new candidate), fashions his wandering hero after the legendary Ulysses, yet he does not make systematic use of Homer's plot as later writers, from Gracián to Joyce, were to do. Reinoso's decision, therefore, to base part of his narrative on that of another is quite unusual even for his age of experimentation. Writers had made use of the classics for didactic purposes—*Ovide Moralisé* comes to mind—but no one had thought of elaborating an existing work into a fiction of one's own. Perhaps Reinoso's training as a poet led him to this creative act, for it is as if Tatius' romance serves him as the basis for his gloss.

15 Bataillon, "Alonso Núñez de Reinoso et les marranes portugais," was the first to point out the gender reversal in *Clareo y Florisea*, where the narrator and almost all the female characters are, in reality, men.

writing, to provide those in her native land with knowledge of her movements and to counsel others in similar circumstances not to imitate her action, not to leave home. While those around her in her island retreat participate in the peaceful pastoral life, she remains a figure apart who, in this *locus amœnus*, sits and weeps as she responds to her own interior landscape, to memory.[16] Although the pastoral world cannot release her from her sorrows, it does offer her a temporary refuge from her troubles; it is a static world where men are not subject to the mutability of fortune. There is no action in this bucolic setting. All events governed by fortune have taken place in the past and have led to Isea's profoundly unhappy state. Novelistically, the past is supplied by episodes drawn from Tatius' narrative; Isea's life was one of constant motion as she fled from one country to another and suffered countless reversals at the hands of adverse fortune.

The Isea (or Melitte, as she was called) whom Reinoso encountered in Tatius' work was neither the narrator nor the heroine. Rather, she was a secondary figure, the conniving, sensuous other woman who pursued the hero Clitophon during his separation from his beloved Leucippe. Reinoso completely transformed Melitte, making her the object of the reader's pity and placing her at the center of the story, for his long-suffering lady participates in both parts of the book, in the maritime episodes transposed from Tatius' tale and in the original chivalric adventures of the knight errant Felesindos, which Isea observes and records.[17] But whether she is recounting her own adventures or those of others, Isea remains the focus of the reader's attention; Reinoso's romance is the story of her endless flight from adverse fortune. As Isea

---

[16] In *La soledad en la poesía española* (Madrid: Revista de Occidente, 1941), Karl Vossler discusses the role of memory in the pastoral.

[17] I do not deal with the chivalric adventures, which in any case lack generic novelty, because Isea is still in motion, thus duplicating her situation in the Byzantine portion. See note 8 above for the identification of "Felesindos" with Feliciano de Silva, who also participated in these experiments in narrative prose. As I indicated in *Alonso Núñez de Reinoso*, p. 30, n. 22, Silva had included in his *Florisel de Niquea* a pastoral episode dealing with "Darinel" (cf. Reinoso's poem No. 6 "Por Delia si hermosa cruel / Murió el pastor Darinel"). See also Sydney Cravens' *Feliciano de Silva y los antecedentes de la novela pastoril en sus libros de caballerías* (Chapel Hill: Estudios de Hispanófila, 1976).

herself comments: "[mi libro] cuenta fortunas ajenas, porque mejor se vea cuán grandes fueron las mías" (433a).[18]

What Reinoso saw in *Clitophon and Leucippe* was the constant motion and the part played by adverse fortune. By linking sequential events through the figure of the unfortunate Isea, he gave his own work internal unity in tone, action, and theme. To advance the theme of fortune, he seized upon the fact that the Byzantine romance's setting is the sea and that its characters are beset by numerous storms and shipwrecks. The sea as metaphor unites theme and action through the repetitive disasters which it supplies. The significance of the sea is not lost upon the book's fictional beings, who comment freely upon the association of the sea with fortune. To unite the theme of fortune to his own subjective agonies, Reinoso makes use of Ovid's *Tristia*. Ovid's poem stands as the model, sine qua non, for Renaissance writers in exile, as the Roman records the storms which beset him on his journey to the far shores of the Black Sea. Significantly, his poem is the ship which sails forth upon the sea of fortune, like a created fictive life.

The Byzantine romance offered to Reinoso, then, the possibility of expressing enforced exile, wanderings, and travail, and of describing lives adversely affected by the capricious goddess. Accordingly, in the segment based on Tatius' work, fortune is blamed for the reversals of fate befalling the central characters: Clareo (Clitophon) believes that his beloved has been killed and that her headless body has been thrown into the sea, and he is subsequently jailed, brought to trial, and sentenced for the supposed crime; Florisea (Leucippe) is abducted, almost loses her virtue, narrowly escapes death, and is held in servitude; Isea (Melitte), apparently widowed when her husband is reported lost at sea, loses the affection of her second husband, Clareo, who accuses her of complicity in the "death" of Florisea, for which crime she also is imprisoned, and although she regains her freedom with the miraculous reappearance of Florisea, she loses Clareo's love definitively when the young lovers are reunited and then joined in marriage.

---

[18] The prose quotations are from the only edition of the work printed in Spain, that of Carlos Aribau in *La novela anterior a Cervantes*, BAE, 3 (Madrid: Rivadeneyra, 1846), pp. 431-68. In "La disposición temporal en el *Lazarillo de Tormes*," *Hispanic Review*, 35 (1957), 264-79, Claudio Guillén demonstrates that "adversidades" and "fortunas" are synonymous.

To these episodes, Reinoso adds losses of his own invention: Isea loses her companions and money in a shipwreck, is captured by pirates and jailed a second time, and at the end of the tale, passes solitary days, friendless in a foreign land. Reinoso, in his desire to elaborate upon Tatius' original, has drawn upon Petrarch's *De remediis utriusque fortunae:* "De la servitud," "De la pérdida del dinero," "De la muger robada por fuerza," "De la infamia," "De la muerte del amigo," "De la ausencia de los amigos," "Del naufragio o peligro del mar," "De la cárcel," "Del destierro," "De la muerte antes de tiempo," are the appropriate chapter headings for the appropriated novelistic events.[19]

Just as he had seen a correspondence between events in his own life and those in *Clitophon and Leucippe,* Núñez de Reinoso used his life as the source of new material to be interpolated in the Byzantine section of his narrative: Isea's stay on the Insula de la Vida refers to the time Reinoso spent with Micas in the Dukedom of Ferrara where Ercole de Este (Duque de Atenas in the episode) welcomed them to his court; the incident in which Isea, as the aftermath of another shipwreck, is detained by the authorities, cast into prison, and accused of traveling with brigands, relates to Reinoso's arrival in either Portugal or the Low Countries in the company of known Judaizers; Isea's subsequent release from jail and employment in the household of a powerful stranger, "el Gran Señor," recounts Reinoso's employment in the Nasi (Mendes-Micas) household; and a pastoral interlude which Isea spends in the company of two sisters and which is interrupted by death is a direct reference to Reinoso's friendship with Sá de Miranda and Ribeiro, "et in Arcadia ego." Undoubtedly, Alonso Núñez de Reinoso, like his fictional creation, felt himself to be the victim of adverse fortune.

[19] Quoted from *De los remedios contra la prospera y adversa fortuna* (Valladolid, 1510). The translator, Francisco de Madrid, was himself a *converso.* In *The Art of the Celestina* (Madison: University of Wisconsin, 1954) and in "The Fall of Fortune: From Allegory to Fiction," *Filologia Romanza,* 4 (1957), 337-54, Stephen Gilman illustrates the importance of the theme to another *converso,* Fernando de Rojas. Although Stanislav Zimic, in "Alonso Núñez de Reinoso, traductor de *Leucipe y Clitofonte,*" *Symposium,* 21 (1967), 166-75, maintains that Reinoso made use of a complete version of Tatius' romance (1550) in order to supplement his list of disasters and to advance the plot, the argument is not convincing. Given his usual candor, why would Reinoso, who readily reveals his principal and secondary sources, conceal this supposed source?

Isea views fortune as an abstract force which holds complete sovereignty over her life and which has singled her out for an unhappy lot in this world. In Reinoso's romance there is no attempt to affix guilt in order to explain her fall from fortune in accordance with Christian beliefs. Neither original sin nor any of the subsequent causal arguments have any bearing on the outcome of the events.[20] Isea, the victim, is quite blameless; there is no hint that she is in any way responsible for her own misfortune. For the explanation, one must look elsewhere.

A key passage, essential for understanding Isea's fate, the work as a whole, and its relevance to the author's life, contains a lengthy commentary on the effects of envy. The scene is a confrontation between Isea and her long-lost husband, but the circumstances neither call for nor measure up to the virulence of the words employed, for Isea is merely trying to appease her irate husband, who has returned to find her involved in a seemingly adulterous relationship. In Tatius' work, Melitte was plainly lying, for she had seduced Clitophon, but in Reinoso's version, Isea is technically telling the truth, for her marriage to Clareo, despite her desires, remains unconsummated. The passage soon veers off course as its author forgets what is appropriate to a Byzantine romance. In fact, he becomes so preoccupied with his personal message that he quite loses the thread of his argument and the events which precipitated the crisis. Leaving behind literary imitation and the fictional situation, Reinoso, through the voice of his narrator, lays the blame for past and present marital ills on "envidia" and launches a virulent attack on the *malsín*:

> ...destruyen hoy día a muchos, porque si un falso, con *falsa acusación* acusa a uno delante de su señor o delante de su príncipe, y trata mal dél, suele imprimir tanto aquella falsa y perversa acusación, que aunque después el pobre acusado se quiera defender o desculpar, no le aprovecha...lo cual no es justo:...*envidia...es destrucción de las honras*, y causa que la virtud

---

20 Although certain segments of *Clareo y Florisea* read like the debates in Responsa literature, there is no indication that Isea's exile is divine punishment meted out for idolatry, in execution of the sentence voiced in Deuteronomy 28: 64-65. Núñez de Reinoso, however, may have turned away from *his* God. He seems to have belonged to that group of agnostic New Christians created by the Inquisition, truly secular beings in the humanistic tradition.

no sea honrada, ni los virtuosos favorecidos, ni los grandes
vistos ni conocidos; y el mal es que la envidia roe y come a los
ánimos de los envidiosos;... *esta envidia reina más contra los grandes*, y
en las casas grandes, *destruyéndolas y despedazándolas*, y *poniéndolas en
pleitos, discordias, trabajos, desventuras, poco o ningún reposo ni sosiego*, es
causa de que *muchos bajos suban* y otros de mayor suerte anden
abatidos.... Y ansí yo creo bien que algún envidioso, porque nos
vio valer y subir, por destruir esta nuestra casa y abajalla...ha
metido discordia y odio entre nosotros.   (448a, emphasis mine)

Now, neither Tatius nor his translators had made reference to
envy as a motivating factor, nor do the fictional circumstances
justify such a digression or sustain the charge. Within the context
of Reinoso's romance, it is patently ridiculous to suggest that
someone, envious of their marital bliss and their social position,
has launched a campaign against them; theirs is hardly the perfect
marriage, nor has their behavior been exactly exemplary. Lexical
emphasis, the reiterated outburst against "un falso, con falsa
acusación," indicates that Reinoso's is more than the standard
complaint against envious fortune for the leveling of estates, and
his charge invites further interpretation.

    Américo Castro supplies the key for comprehending Isea's
outburst. During the period of his American exile, don Américo
formulated his theory of the "realidad" of Spanish history and
suggested that certain recurring terms, such as "envidia," "honra,"
"reposo," and "sosiego," held special significance for Golden Age
Spain, meanings which sprang from the tensions of the times.[21]
Such is Núñez de Reinoso's application of the words; he has
hispanized Isea's defense. Reinoso has supplied the legal consequences of envious attacks, "pleitos"; recorded the emotional response, "ningún reposo"; and related the total situation to the
"destrucción de las honras." Thus, the digressive diatribe, which
does little to advance the plot, supplies the cause of Isea's eventual
and otherwise inexplicable fall from fortune, a fall which has no
basis in the action. The passage also reveals the reasons for
Reinoso's leaving Spain, for it would seem to summarize the
agonizing existence of the Spanish *converso*, falsely accused, denounced to the authorities, embroiled in legal battles, threatened
in a thousand ways, and living in dread of the consequences.

---

[21] *España en su historia (Cristianos, moros y judíos)*, (Buenos Aires: Losada,
1948) and its subsequent reworkings.

Following this impassioned plea, Isea's husband disappears, without much ado, from the book, and without even taking note of his absence, she feels compelled to move on, for reasons which she does not express. Later, after suffering fresh maritime disasters, she decides to continue her journey by land: "acordé de hacer mi camino por tierra, por andar tan cansada de la fastidiosa mar" (454a). Although the change of venue allows the author to introduce his chivalric tale, his fictional creation fares no better on land than on the sea: "peregrina, perdida, acosada y estranjera" (453b), the "sin ventura" Isea continues her restless wanderings, forever pursued by adverse fortune.

As a class or caste, none felt more subject to the whims of the fickle goddess than did Spain's *conversos*, who displayed inordinate interest in the theme of fortune. The Holy Office itself felt compelled to censure heretical references to the term "fortuna" expressed by dissident thinkers who, influenced by Judaic philosophy, maintained that divine providence did not extend to the sublunary world where fortune, or blind chance, regulated men's lives and where survival was based on their ability to overcome adverse circumstances.[22] It is, therefore, doubly ironic that in their secularization of the term, New Christian authors used "fortuna" as a euphemism for the Inquisition, as Stephen Gilman has indicated, a reading sustained by Juan Vives' quiet comment to a friend: "La Fortuna continúa siendo igual y fiel a sí misma contra mi padre, contra todos los míos y aún contra mí mismo."[23] So it was with Núñez de Reinoso. In his blending of fact and fiction, Reinoso created a surrogate self who is a "peregrina,"[24] a wanderer

[22] Charles Fraker, "The Importance of Pleberio's Soliloquy," *Romanische Forschungen*, 77 (1966), 515-29, suggests that such a view of the world derives from Maimonides.

[23] "The *Conversos* and the Fall of Fortune," *Collected Studies in Honor of Américo Castro's Eightieth Year* (Oxford, 1965), 127-36, at p. 131. The quotation appears on p. 551 of Américo Castro's *La realidad histórica de España* (México: Porrúa, 1954).

[24] Neither Reinoso nor his fictional stand-in is related to the devout pilgrim about whom Antonio Vilanova writes in "El peregrino andante en el *Persiles* de Cervantes," *Boletín de la Real Academia de Buenas Letras de Barcelona*, 22 (1949), 97-159. For a definition of the term in context, as used by Reinoso and other exiles, see my book, especially the section called "The Travails of a *peregrino*," pp. 125-28.

in flight from her homeland, an outcast without honor in her native land, an exile pursued by a relentless foe, the Inquisition in the guise of Fortune.

From his Venetian haven, Reinoso composed a fictional journal which is the factual catalogue of his misfortunes.[25] Counterposing two Renaissance attitudes, the contemplative and the active, he chose to express the present through the soothing, static pastoral,[26] and to express the past through the turbulent Byzantine mode. In selecting as his "agonist" a woman who cannot oppose fortune with "virtù," a masculine quality, he rejected the possibility of the requisite happy ending,[27] and by fashioning a fictional character who does not combat adversity, thereby restoring her honor, he set forth the dilemma of the ordinary *converso* to whom greatness of spirit was lacking and final triumph denied.

Reinoso composed his *roman à clef* for a group of "enterados," whose lives, like his own, had been touched by the workings of the Holy Office. He wrote for Juan Micas and his circle in Italy and for friends in the Iberian Peninsula, for those who had fled their native land and for those who, despite the odds, had chosen to stay. Although *Clareo y Florisea* is the account of one (wo)man's personal suffering, surely it reflects a collective experience in which fellow *conversos* could see, as Reinoso had seen in Tatius' work, that the fictional situations were remarkably analogous to the historical predicament which they were living and through which their ancestors had lived. For this "minoría selecta," such Byzantine "histories" geographically and temporally linked the Second Diaspora with the First as cyclic events.[28]

[25] For those interested in autobiography as a literary form, consult Philippe Lejeune, *Le Pacte autobiographique* (Paris: Editions du Seuil, 1975), and Georges May, *L'Autobiographie* (Paris: Presses Universitaires de France, 1979).

[26] In the pastoral episode of Edmund Spenser's *Faerie Queene* (Book VI, ix-x), for example, the knight errant Calidor charges into the bucolic setting, mounted on a steed and sweating. All this activity is out of place in the pastoral world, and it is incumbent upon Calidor to dismount and rest so that he may contemplate his situation.

[27] *Clareo y Florisea* is one of the works treated by Manuel Ferrer-Chivite in "Notas sobre la anagnórisis como procedimiento marginalizante," *Imprévue*, Suppl. 1 (1980-81), 32-58.

[28] Núñez de Reinoso's conversion of a fictional story into a personal history is somewhat akin to the problems which William Nelson examines

Clareo y Florisea clearly belongs to the creative impulse of the first half of the sixteenth century, to that period of intense literary activity, dramatic as well as novelistic, inspired in the tension of the times, when content found and shaped the forms.[29] The concerns of the later post-Tridentine romance were primarily aesthetic; neither inspiration, tone, nor aim was the same in the age of imitation, when authors elaborated the forms forged by those earlier innovators. As a precursor, Alonso Núñez de Reinoso's contribution to the creation of the novel, for all times, rests solidly on three facts: 1. he adapted an already existing work of fiction to write one of his own; 2. he considered his own life worthy of record; and 3. he experimented with the newly-evolving narrative modes. The man was modest; his achievement, stunning.

NORTHEASTERN UNIVERSITY

in *Fact or Fiction: The Dilemma of the Renaissance Storyteller* (Cambridge: Harvard, 1973). In a forthcoming article, "La voluntad de la leyenda de Miguel de Luna," *Nueva Revista de Filología Hispánica*, Francisco Márquez Villanueva exposes that author's deliberate flight to fancy in *Historia verdadera del rey don Rodrigo*. But rather than writing fictionalized history, Reinoso embarked on what might be termed the creation of an allusive historical fiction. Consciousness of their plight may have induced in *converso* and *morisco* authors alike the sense of their place in time necessary for essaying the historical novel long before Lukács discerns its presence in the industrial age.

[29] It is worth noting that in the creation-conscious group formed by Reinoso, Ribeiro, Sá de Miranda, and Montemayor, pastoral prose fiction developed hand-in-hand with their pastoral poetry.

The Critic as Witness for the Prosecution: Resting the Case Against Lázaro de Tormes

GEORGE A. SHIPLEY

RONIC LITERATURE IS recursive, it requires re-reading, it depends on rereading for its completion. Autobiographical narratives are bound more closely to the present than to the past: "now," and for the purposes of "now" (be those purposes public or private), the autobiographer orders time and experience, discovering, recreating, devising patterns of significance that are such, fully and for the first time, only "now". A fiction, then, that is both ironic and autobiographical stands doubly in need of rereadings of an active, systematic kind that give careful consideration to the text's patterns and the reader's experience of them, and also to the relation of both of these to the needs and purposes of the writers, both the author of the fiction and his narrator. The understanding of these inter-related aspects of design and meaning requires that the text be studied, like a Garcilaso sonnet, backwards and forwards.[1] Having

---

[1] The comparison of *Lazarillo*'s intense organization to that of a sonnet was drawn first by Francisco Rico, in his valuable *La novela picaresca*

read Lázaro's claims, the first and forward act, the reader is
challenged (by the nature of the fiction and, remotely, by its
author) to read the text *as* a set of claims, and this we can do best
by backward accounting.

I. *"Cuando me paro a contemplar mi estado"*

When we look backward with Lázaro from the narrator's
situation—which he sketches elliptically and allusively in Tratado
VII and in his Prologue—and attempt to contemplate along with
him his way out of the worrisome isolation in which he stands, we
come to see that his problem is in one respect startlingly similar to
that of his anonymous creator. Both are innovative designers of
autobiographical fictions. Lázaro seeks to reaffirm damaged links
to his community by asserting and representing the underlying
likeness of human beings through society and across time. To that
end he assembles a pastiche of experience and invention that well
might gain for him the re-integration and renewed social security
he desires, if the common denominator of likeness he claims to
share with his *conciudadanos* is anywhere near as base as he ("con-
fesando yo no ser más sancto que mis vecinos" [6]) depicts it to be.
If his text wins sufficient support by convincing, and more likely
by intimidating and by entertaining his readers (that is, the fictional readers identified in his Prologue, including Vuestra Merced), he will perhaps achieve assimilation at last and as much
material and sensual bliss as he has dared covet.

Lázaro's set of claims, once it is regarded as such, is as specious
as before (so long as we looked on it as a narrative) it was
entertaining. A backward review reveals what the well-told tale
conceals.

First, Tratado VII. The final *tratado* is rich in inferences, as
Harry Sieber has shown, but poor in information.[2] No doubt such
an engaging and expressive writer as Lázaro could do better, or

y el punto de vista (Barcelona: Seix Barral, 1970), at pp. 31-33. The text of
La vida de Lazarillo de Tormes, y de sus fortunas y adversidades from which I shall
quote is also Rico's, included in his *La novela picaresca española*, I (Barcelona:
Planeta, 1967). This essay concludes a line of argument begun in "The
Critic as Witness for the Prosecution: Making the Case Against Lázaro
de Tormes," *PMLA*, 97 (1982), 179-94.

    2 See chapter VII of Harry Sieber's *Language and Society in "La vida de
Lazarillo de Tormes"* (Baltimore: Johns Hopkins Univ. Press, 1978).

could at least do more. He does not respond adequately to the mandate that he "escriba y relate el caso muy por extenso" (7). This climactic phase of his life (*cumbre?* catastrophe?), which is of central interest to his first reader, comprises but 4.7% of his studied recollections.[3] It barely represents Lázaro as stable, useful, and properly unctuous in the Toledo community, and as subordinate, powerless, and submissive in the intimate sphere (or rather triangle) that most intrigues his neighbors and his readers: he consents to marriage, accepts his superior's advice, cowers before his wife, and blinds and deafens himself.

Tratados VI-IV: (Remember, we are now regarding the text retrospectively from the narrator's situation, attempting to gain an imaginative entry into that situation, in order to study the narrator's way of plotting his escape from it.) These are for Lázaro a risk worth creating. Two snippets and a brief chapter (1%, .6%, and 10.7% of his text) dilute the present *caso* by associating with it a rich local history of perverted dalliance and malfeasance extending beyond the city walls and backward for something over four years' time. The danger to Lázaro of self-incrimination is lessened by the narrator's reticence, by his poses of innocence, by the "back-grounding" of himself and "highlighting" of other ne'er-do-wells, and by coded allusions to his own previous infamy (*zapatos, cosillas, panderos, moler,* etc.) that are more likely to amuse than to enrage anyone sufficiently knowing to comprehend them. And, what is more, this first extension of the scene and history of the *caso* makes possible a further and more useful extension.

Tratados III-I: These chapters carry to their inclusive limits the narrator's claims of full disclosure, for they take in all the remaining time and space Lázaro has inhabited. Within such generous bounds he has room in which to maneuver unrestrained. Far from Toledo and the scrutiny of Vuestra Merced, Lazarillo can be portrayed quite plausibly as a victim of that incapacitating social malady Américo Castro called hereditary determinism.[4] Lázaro can

---

[3] Following is the line count (and corresponding percentages) for the several divisions in Lázaro's *Vida* (lines containing but a single word are dropped): Prologue: 44 lines (2.3%); Tr. 1: 467 (24.4); Tr. 2: 417 (21.8); Tr. 3: 661 (34.5); Tr. 4: 12 (.6); Tr. 5: 206 (10.7); Tr. 6: 20 (1.0); Tr. 7: 90 (4.7); total: 1917 lines. Trs. I-III constitute 80.6% of the text and 82.5% of the seven Tratados.

[4] "Perspectiva de la novela picaresca," in *Hacia Cervantes,* 3rd ed. (Madrid: Taurus, 1967), pp. 118-42, at pp. 124-25.

both suggest that he has been deformed and thwarted by un-
manageable causes and conditions, and claim for himself a decent
motive, resistent will, and rare constancy in acting in accordance
with his mother's exhortation ("Procura de ser bueno..." [13],
echoed when he claims his triumph: "...todos mis trabajos y
fatigas hasta entonces pasados fueron pagados con *alcanzar lo que
procuré*, que fue un oficio real..." [72]). Onto the same *tabula rasa*,
which Francisco Márquez Villanueva calls the blank check of
readers' sympathy that Lázaro will bounce when he reaches maturity, the narrator inscribes the ugly portraits of his first masters,
insinuates their correspondence to three degraded estates, and so
undermines generally his superiors' grounds for acting superior.[5]

Readers disposed to take Lázaro at his word and, consequently,
to harbor an opinion of the narrator more forgiving than mine
may wish to raise two objections here. First, if, as I claim, Lázaro
enlarges his account to include Tratados I-III because the time and
space represented therein are his to mould freely to his advantage,
why does he include in Tratado I damning details concerning his
mother's wantonness and his father's crimes, conviction, and exile? Would he, a rascal intent on rising, currying favor, seeking
fame, not more likely conceal such shameful origins and claim
another more promising? Two lines of reply occur to me. Lázaro's
claim to have *risen* to his present position, a proposition which the
powerful in Toledo would find laughingly absurd and in no way
challenging, rests logically on his having come up to his present
low station from the very basement of society, where prostitutes,
thieves, moriscos, and other rabble live and multiply like rats.
Acknowledging or inventing this primal shame fits the narrator's
needs and purposes. Then too we could reason, without forcing
this stylized and ironic fiction into the tradition of nineteenth-
century documentary realism, that Lázaro (and also the squire of
Tratado III) live in a world, like their author's, obsessed with
genealogy and family origins, the falsification of these, and their
legal verification in a wide range of cases pending adjudication or
merely attracting the curiosity of society's several sorts of judges.

___

   [5] "Sebastián de Horozco y el Lazarillo de Tormes," *Revista de Filología
Española*, 41 (1957), at pp. 292-93: "...Lazarillo, niño precoz, avispado y
listo, después de ganarse—cheque en blanco—nuestra simpatía, nos
defrauda escandalosamente al llegar a la edad adulta convertido en un
ser abyecto."

And no place showed more interest in such matters than Toledo, for generations a magnet for true and false nobles and a rack for true and false Christians, who often found themselves damned if they did and damned if they did not conceal their family histories. If Lázaro's narrative is anything close to being a deposition, or the narrator has any reason to anticipate his involvement in a legal process, he would know from the common experience of others— including some of those whose shame he, as official crier, had proclaimed—the danger and probable futility of grafting the lowest branches of his family tree. The processes of justice were repressive in the society upon which Lázaro's is modeled, and the centers of power cooperated efficiently against threats. Lázaro might choose to reveal his base parentage rather than risk the revelations that would follow a Toledo official's routine inquiry to his Salamanca counterparts concerning the family history of the scion of Tomé González and Antona Pérez.[6]

As for a second possible objection: the fact that the scene of Tratado III is Toledo may seem to contradict my claim that Tratados I-III constitute a falsification of Lázaro's past achieved by an imaginative rendering of matters beyond Vuestra Merced's oversight. But the squire, who is in Toledo, is not of Toledo. He is desperately intent on playing a categorical role, and he represents a national problem; nothing about him is distinctively Toledan. He has no name; he has distanced himself from his origins and quite likely he has falsified them; he has no friends (52,58); he has no

---

[6] An instructive example of such institutional cooperation in the pursuit of "truth" surfaces in the experience of Antonio de Medrano, who, in Toledo, 1530, was tortured by Inquisition interrogators seeking to incriminate him in a scandalous nest of heterodox practices. Within a few days of the torture, information exacted from that poor soul was transmitted, precisely to Salamanca, and introduced deviously into another proceeding, the trial of Francisca Hernández; the Salamanca court's findings were then promptly reapplied to Medrano and dutifully entered into the Toledo records of his *caso*. See Angela Selke de Sánchez, "El caso del bachiller Antonio de Medrano, iluminado epicúreo del siglo XVI, " *Bulletin Hispanique*, 58 (1956), 408, n. 21. For more on witty literary reflections of justice in this period, see Stephen Gilman, "Matthew 5:10 in Castilian Jest and Earnest," *Studia Hispanica in honorem R. Lapesa*, I (Madrid, 1972), 257-65; and on the hidden costs of institutionalizing dogmatic justice, see Gilman's "The Case of Diego Alonso: Hypocrisy and the Spanish Inquisition," *Daedalus*, 108, No. 3 (1979), 135-44.

traceable past and no history subsequent to his flight from the bill-
collectors. These latter come to recognize full well that he is a
fraud living behind a façade, and they laugh off their loss (65).
Toledo, their reaction implies, is full of his sort. The squire, we
might say, is an effective "transition figure" *for the narrator.*
Through him Lázaro completes, in Tratado III, his comprehensive
representation of general social decadence (three masters who
bring to mind the three estates) and articulates it with the particular scene of Lazarillo's confirmatory experiences, the Toledo of
Vuestra Merced, the "malas lenguas, que nunca faltaron ni fal-
tarán" (73), and Lázaro's first readers.

This backward view, from over Lázaro's shoulder, of the design
he created fosters our recognition of the great distance the narrator contrived to put between himself "now" and that diminutive
Lazarillo whose apparent innocence initially, and developing wit
afterwards, catch and hold the reader's attention *and his sympathy*
for most of the duration of his reading. If, understanding the
narrator's ruse, we eliminate from view all this contrived context
and focus—as Vuestra Merced ordered Lázaro to do—on the here
and now of the narrator, and take in only what we see before us in
the manner a clear-seeing neighbor might, we will regard at last
the ugly picture that Lázaro attempted to reduce to a mere detail
in a blighted urban landscape: the picture of a complaisant cuckold,
or better (for being less relaxed and genteel than that formula), a
pimp and confidence-man of glib tongue and fast hands who is also
a desperate materialist equipped with neither ethical nor moral
resources for defending himself from his *fortunas y adversidades,* the
renewed buffeting that threatens to blow him out to sea.

II. *Lázaro's perversion of humor and comedy*

Lázaro has other resources for his defense, however, of a kind
not previously utilized by those of his condition. And with them—
that is, with pen and paper—his hand, tongue, and lively imagination conspire to fashion a novel defense that, at least among
readers *outside* the fictional world, has proved spectacularly and

enduringly successful.[7] We are greatly entertained by the texture of this funny book. Laughter reverberates through Lazarillo's world and outward into ours: characters laugh, and why not? It's very funny. Lazarillo laughs, Lázaro laughs, and Lázaro induces his readers to laugh, and why not? It's all very funny. It is a masterpiece of humor and comic design representing the narrator's risky but exceedingly amusing solution to the problem of leveling with his readers. No tool blurs distinctions and reminds us of our fundamental alikeness more efficiently than laughter. A sharp awareness of the socializing force of laughter—its power to promote a sense of community among those who can be enlisted to laugh *with* him and to define and isolate deviants and their behavior by training laughter *at* them—is developed by Lazarillo in the course of his apprenticeship and manifested fully by Lázaro the master craftsman of his *tour de force artistique*.[8] There is a bit of the court jester in our town crier, who is knowing and feigns simplicity, flaunts his deformity and claims powerful protection, endures ridicule and shames his accusers.

All this he does, and more, so amusingly that it would seem mean of his readers to do to him (that is, to imagine doing to him) what we might deem thoroughly justified if we had against him only a bare list of the charges he concedes in his deposition, or if we were to base a finding of justice on the evidence of the *caso* alone. While we are being amused, we are not apt to think of Lázaro's humorous and comic strategy as a preferred choice selec-

---

[7] It whetted the interest of an Alemán, a Quevedo, a Cervantes, in novel defenses and, through them and others, had inestimable effects on the rest of us readers. And this because, though novel, it is primitive only in being original and radical; otherwise it is sufficiently finished, whole, and persuasive to do still what it was styled—by its narrator—to do four centuries ago: that is, to delight many, please others, and defend the fox from the hounds.

[8] In each of the first three *tratados* Lazarillo is depicted as the butt of humor and as acutely aware of its function as a reinforcing mechanism for symbolic isolation (20, 24, 25; 41; 58, 65). In Tratado V he has become one of the laughers, and the simple faithful are the isolated objects (73-74). In Tratado VII *malas lenguas* threaten to sever Lázaro's ties to the community. To arrest their laughter and his backsliding, he becomes the genial laugh-maker we know, and confirms in his art both the socializing power of laughter and our suspicion that he is tapping it to stave off dreadful isolation from the community. His funny book is, as Kenneth Burke would say, equipment for living.

ted *by the narrator* from among options. When we move on from reading and laughing to the rereading the text invites (and which it also rewards, as every experienced reader of irony anticipates it will, by eliciting, among other responses, renewed and more intense laughter) and come to recognize the tactics of falsification I have pointed to above, we are moved further to question the values invested in Lázaro's chosen devices and to contrast his choices with available options he did not elect.

A number of options might be suggested to us by our own experience of the world, including the literary experience we bring to bear on this speculation. Coincidence among readers, at this point, is neither likely nor desirable, and there is no need to list options or to weigh possible strategies for rewriting the fiction. We will certainly agree that Lázaro's tale could be written differently, and remember that it has been rewritten so frequently and variously as to constitute a rich literary genre and to reveal a persistently significant myth.[9] There is nothing unusual in the spilling forth of blood, tears, and vomit in this familiar story. Nor in the narrator's recording his throbbing pain, cramped intestines, bruised skull, lacerated gums, and other violations of his body. Nor in the negative emotions, principally fear, shame, and despair, awakened by such experiences. What is novel and arresting in this account, and never will be repeated in quite Lázaro's way, and therefore defines the peculiarity of Lázaro's relation to his fictional world, is the tone of the narrator's recollections. He represents Lazarillo's victimization over the years, at the hands of many repulsive masters, *without* the resentment, rancor, rage, and revulsion his experiences justify. Lazarillo's pain does not pain Lázaro, or the reader. It affords us pleasure. We are not moved to share imaginatively the youngster's experience of fear, shame and despair (except, fleetingly, in Tratado III, where rereaders suspect the protagonist's emotions are counterfeit).[10] These negative reactions of the subject are long gone; Lázaro leaves them behind in the

---

[9] See Claudio Guillén, "Toward a Definition of the Picaresque," pp. 71-106 in his *Literature as System* (Princeton: Princeton Univ. Press, 1971), and Alexander Blackburn, *The Myth of the Picaro* (Chapel Hill: Univ. of North Carolina Press, 1979).

[10] Several scholars—notably María Rosa Lida de Malkiel and Francisco Ayala (see the latter's *El "Lazarillo": Nuevo examen de algunos aspectos* [Madrid: Taurus, 1971], pp. 60-61), and Angel González Palencia, *Del "Lazarillo" a Quevedo* (Madrid: CSIC, 1946), p. 20—find Lazarillo's naive

distant "Early Years". The narrator shows no sympathy for his teacher, the blind seer who bleeds while his lazarus taunts him and scampers away (27). Neither does he give evidence of any impulse to clear the temple of priests of the kind he encountered in Maqueda and in Toledo. Nor to follow after the impoverished squire who, he claims, so touched him with compassion that he fed him scraps he had begged for himself; on the contrary, seeking out that ignoble wretch in his recollections, he inflicts a mean stylistic injury on him.[11] We could not expect Lázaro to call for the

fear of death hard to accept in light of his previous experiences in a hard world. I question also (below, note 11), along with L. J. Woodward ("Author-Reader Relationship in the Lazarillo del [sic] Tormes," *Forum for Modern Language Studies,* I [1965], 43-53) and others, the charitable nature of his sharing with the squire. Frank Durand, in "The Author and Lázaro: Levels of Comic Meaning," *Bulletin of Hispanic Studies,* 45 (1968), 89-101, esp. at pp. 94-96, rightly stresses Lázaro's ability as a clever teller of tales. Durand notes the "dichotomy" between "event and recital of it, which enables [Lázaro] to transform a horrible experience into a most entertaining anecdote...; the description of the event itself lacks bitterness and is detached." The result: "good humour [?] and almost constant laughter provoked in author, narrator and reader."

  11 There is no Christian love either in Lazarillo's treatment of the squire or in Lázaro's retelling of it. Only in a loose sense, devoid of generosity and moral distinction, is there any "charity" in Lazarillo's giving. Feigning sickliness and acting pious, Lazarillo quickly begged six *libras* of bread, ate four of them, and returned home with some additional scraps of meat (51). Before the starving squire he conceals his earlier snack, chews deliberately at the leavings, prolongs his master's suffering past the point of cruelty before tossing him a bone and bread. Lázaro, years later, stresses the meanness of the interaction, not the giving. A primitive animal instinct is at work here, in both actors. Lazarillo shares in the fashion one carnivore, dominant and sated, finally will allow another, famished, to approach the carcass of its kill. Animal imagery, in fact, is much in evidence in this passage, as Alan Deyermond observes (in *Lazarillo de Tormes, a Critical Guide* [London: Grant & Cutler, 1975], p. 69). The squire paces nervously, his eyes lowered submissively and fastened onto the food, while Lazarillo feeds alone ("comienzo a cenar y *morder* en *mis tripas* y pan"; "comencé a comer, y él *se andaba paseando*") and eyes his adversary cunningly in return. Then, filled and affirmed in his dominance, "Póngole en *las uñas* la otra...." The squire, still submissive, grovels for his bone: "*asentóseme al lado* y comienza a comer..., *royendo cada huesecillo...* mejor que *un galgo...*" (52-53). It is doubtful that the protagonist felt charitable; it is certain that the narrator does not. (For quite a different view of this matter, see Joseph V. Ricapito's "Introducción" to his edition of *Lazarillo de Tormes* [Madrid: Cátedra, 1977], at p. 74).

reordering of society (a notion that would be for him both anachronistic and counterproductive), but we can imagine him execut-
ing a strategy that would add to his recognition of social decay a
call to restore the fallen order (a "conservative" ploy consistent
with his interests and unobjectionable in theory to his betters, the
naturally superior). Lázaro makes no such appeal; nor does he,
despite—or because of?—his years in the company of men of the
Word, turn to a god for relief, rescue, or revenge. God's greatest
gift to him having been his wife ("y me hace Dios con ella mil
mercedes" [80]), he holds no illusions concerning His charity.

Such are some of the paths not taken by the narrator in the
course of constructing a bridge outward and backward from his
imprisoning present. A considerable and intriguing past is displayed, but not for the purpose of censure, not for the attachment
of past emotions to the present, and not to document a serious
claim of personal progress or singular exemplarity. What is illus-
trated by the narrator is the assertion of the consistency of his
experience: his own developing self-consistency over time, and the
analogous consistency all across society (horizontally and vertical-
ly) of the selves that together constitute the civil macrocosm. The
narrator arranges a series of claims ("that is the way it happened")
in such a way that its serial momentum and thematic and stylistic
redundancy, achieved mainly in the preponderant Tratados I-III,
come to focus with great persuasive force on the present, com-
manding a general conclusion ("that, in sum, is the way it is")
concerning Lázaro's life that is both comic and humorous.

The *caso* and Lázaro's attendant situation are not extraordinary
or aberrant features of his *Vida*. They complete the coherent
design of the series and both confirm and are confirmed by the
patterns of conduct they bring up to date as well as by stylistic
details that call earlier situations to mind. The completed design,
albeit fragile and deceptive, is comic in that it portrays the protagonist's integration into his community (though we sense that in
truth he remains isolated and that the text is a tense form of
wishful thinking or secular prayer, a "may it be thought so, and
may it go on"). The novice is instructed, tested, and succeeds; he
assimilates what the narrator maintains are society's values and
reaffirms them, first in his way of living and again by proclaiming
them in his writing, which is his credo. He represents the continuity of society, now that he is incorporated, and the merging of
protagonist and narrator completes a process satisfyingly without

terminating it; the text is open-ended (though a vestigial threat to comic solidarity is conjured in the final image and verb tense: "I was at that point on the pinnacle").

Our rereading allows us to see that Lázaro has imposed this comic design on a life that (insofar as we see it represented in his *Vida*) is grotesque and naturally tragic in outline: a history of rejection, isolation, powerlessness, material and spiritual poverty, deprivation, frustration, perversion and emasculation, of alienated being sustained precariously only by willing submission to the needs and demands of others. Not, generally speaking, the stuff of comedy. If it is in this instance, nevertheless, commonly accepted as such, this is due to the artful renaming and recontextualization by which means the narrator converts the *caso* into a laughing matter. Lazarillo experienced at an early age what observers of the social scene lately proclaim as a behavioral principle; that is, "heartily laughing together at the same thing forms an immediate bond, much as enthusiasm for the same ideal does."[12] Lacking positive ideals and encountering (or perceiving) none about him in the community, Lázaro relies on laughter to serve as a substitute bond, producing the sort of "strong fellow feeling among participants"[13]—that is, *among his readers*—that he claims he once observed the blindman and others generate at his expense and for their pleasure. Still the object of derision and aggression in his community, Lázaro makes use of "the protective property of humor" to deflect the attention of his laughing public away from himself here and now.[14] He tells a very funny story about how he

[12] Konrad Lorenz, as quoted by Jacob Levine, ed., in *Motivation in Humor* (New York: Atherton Press, 1969), pp. 12-13. My thanks to Kay Kruger-Hickman for this reference.

[13] Levine, p. 12. Lorenz observes that "laughter, like greeting, tends to create a bond. From self-observation I can safely assert that shared laughter not only diverts aggression but also produces a feeling of social unity" (*On Aggression* [New York: Bantam, 1969], p. 172).

[14] Levine, p. 11: "By formalized joking behavior,...tabood urges are channeled or drained off in acceptable ways.... It is by this protective property of humor that individuals have found immunity from the destructive aggression of others...." Levine quotes Sigmund Freud: "In every epoch of history those who have had something to say but could not say it without peril have eagerly assumed the fool's cap. The audience at whom their forbidden speech was aimed tolerated it more easily if they could at the same time laugh and flatter themselves with the reflection that the unwelcome words were clearly nonsensical."

grew up from being, because of his inexperience and naiveté (the true targets of humorous attack throughout), a victim and humorous object for aggressors and by-standers (Tratados I-III) to become a by-stander himself, amused by the exploitation of others and bound into complicity with the aggressors (Tratado V), and then, in his maturity, an aggressive agent dedicated to satisfying the by-standers (his neighbors, now his readers) with whom he has cemented bonds of common interest. He is a *pregonero* of Toledo, which means that he now makes his living through symbolic aggression, inflicting words of abuse on the community's officially designated victims. But by far the firmest and most satisfying bond Lázaro has forged is the humorous *Vida* itself. It is pointedly aggressive and all-embracing (locating infamous *cosas señaladas* then and now, there and here) in leveling distinctions based on ideal values and in negating all exclusive social bonds except those of laughter. It is also self-confirming in its capacity to move its readers to laughter as they follow the fortunes of a butt of ridicule who becomes a worldly and knowing laugh-master, a verbal wizard intent on providing his readers delight and pleasure (and also provoking acute embarrassment and paralysis of their power in those detractors who recognize themselves targeted in the scene), without reviving their somnolent faculties of moral discrimination.

We have no basis for judging the success of Lázaro's narration among readers in *his* world. We are tempted to imagine a bonanza of laughter accompanying the narrator's safe entry "a buen puerto" (7). In *our* world Lázaro has proved enormously successful in providing pleasure and delight to a wide variety of readers. The near unanimity of response is very nearly laughing confirmation of the Prologue thesis so central to Lázaro's defense: that soldiers, preachers, gentlemen, artists,...and now readers, scholars, critics, and of course Lázaro, are all fundamentally alike. In consequence Lázaro himself has been more often than not practically exonerated of the charges of wrong-doing implicit in his history and excepted from the criticisms he and his readers make of others in his world. This has been so not because the evidence he presents on his own behalf is compelling or because his reasoning sweeps us into assent. More likely it is because, as Lorenz puts it, "barking dogs may occasionally bite, but laughing men hardly ever shoot."[15]

---

[15] Levine, p. 11; Lorenz, p. 285. It will be obvious that I do not

So long as we are kept laughing, we are well-disposed towards the laugh-master; we are in his thrall; we share his assumptions, and even his concept of justice. (Such is the coercive power of humor that Lazarillo, painfully thrashed by the "perverso ciego," nevertheless deems it a "sinjusticia" not to join in the laughter provoked by his master's witty account of their mêlée [24].)

While our laughter symbolizes acceptance of the laugh-master, it is a short-term and partly involuntary show of support and cannot be sustained long enough to constitute a durable comic principle. It is true that the intense humor of Lázaro's *Vida* has secondary, lingering effects on some readers. After laughing long and hard at the text, some are disposed to remember it solely or mainly for its humor, as a funny book (oddly structured, maybe incomplete, but masterfully entertaining). Other readers, however, find that the more they reread, the more additional reactions crowd in to compete with laughter for uppermost control of the imagination, competing in effect with Lázaro for control of the reader's assessment of him and his world.

Lázaro's control of the assessment is broken the moment the reader comes to sense that humor is another of the narrator's (not the author's) weapons, his principal offensive weapon, for opposing the forces of truth and rumor that have isolated him and threaten to drive him out of the community. Take away his humor, interrupt our laughter, and Lázaro's comic counterattack is shattered. The narrator then stands alone again in Toledo, once more a cynical and despicable *cornudo*, and an inviting scapegoat. The reader, ashamed now of his first laughter (evidence that he too has been manipulated by the unworthy narrator), withdraws the imaginative support he was induced to lend Lázaro and to invest in a portrait of society predicated only on a low common

---

subscribe to Frank Durand's view of the function of humor and comedy in *Lazarillo*. For Durand "the end and all important purpose...is to make us laugh..."(p. 90); the author gives us "a total comic view of society" (p. 100, also p. 89); in Tratado VII "the humour of incidents and language so evident throughout the work is...fused with the more serious comic outlook of narrator and 'author' " (p. 101). I maintain that his readers' laughter is for Lázaro a means rather than an end, as is his comic view also—the end in mind being, of course, his self-protection. Lázaro attempts to effect a self-serving fusion of humor and comedy; his author warns us not to be deceived.

denominator of deceit, material satisfaction, and exploitation of the weak and gullible.

Thus reminded of his own weakness and gullibility, craftily exploited by the narrator, the reader may seek remedies both within and beyond the text. Within Lázaro's account of his experience there is no representation of truly resistant comic values in society—nothing enduring, cohesive, incorporative, forgiving. Either such values have little force in his world (which makes it a grotesque place, unfit for living in and laughing at), or their force has not been acknowledged by the narrator (perhaps because to do so would be to undermine his defense and to condemn himself by revealing awareness of higher and more generous standards in others than are manifested in him). Beyond the text lie our own experiences, which may contradict Lázaro's implied assertions. We may have certain knowledge, for example, of spouses who cannot be described as merely "la cosa del mundo que yo más quiero" (89), of gentlemen and others who are not just desperate mimics of the forms of gentility, of clerics and laity and even non-believers who are charitable. Incongruities between our experience and Lázaro's narrative impress on us how very partial, deliberately depressing, and restricted is the world-vision Lázaro put before us, both in the range of human experience it encompasses within it and in the range of emotions it elicits. (Alonso Quijano also suffers pain, fear, and despair, but....) But is it right for us to censure the narrator for his inability or unwillingness to imagine a better way of getting along with his neighbors in Toledo? Is such censure a function of a right reading of La vida de Lazarillo de Tormes? Is it invited by the fiction?

III. Honos alit artes, *sometimes*

Yes, it is. Our rejection of Lázaro and his model of community life may contain elements of personal resistance to such a negative and unprincipled view of things and also resentment that we have been the narrator's dupes, but not all our reactions need be subjective or tied to values outside the text. The anonymous author presiding over his creation and, therefore, over our experience of it seems to keep his distance and to leave his narrator to his own devices. But the author is not beyond planting evidence in his text to signal his disagreement with his principal creature. A case in point is his indirect way of alerting his reader to the need for moral evaluation of what Lázaro puts before us ostensibly to afford us only pleasure and delight.[16] There is other evidence, particularly in Tratado II, as a thorough study of narrator-author relations will show one day. Here, more modestly, we will reconsider only one small and well-known bit of Lázaro's Prologue, a highly significant bit, however, just because it teaches us that the anonymous author of *La vida de Lazarillo de Tormes* urges those who will follow him to reject as false the narrator's version of society. In the terms of his partially-concealed rejection lies a clue as to the nature of the social contract the author might support as an alternative to his creature's declaration of general human deceit and aggressiveness.

"Y a este propósito dice Tulio: 'La honra cría las artes' " (6). Cicero's words were well-known to 16th-century readers,[17] and they remain well-known today, thanks partly to the accident of their prominent appearance in Lázaro's apology. There they follow the narrator's defense of free expression and his plea for a reading, and they precede the three examples of "honorable" activity that parallel and legitimize his own, thereby injecting persuasive classical authority into several lines of argument that stand in need of buttressing. The borrowing is clever, as we might expect of our narrator. Also, it is mistranslated, misconstrued, and recontextualized before our eyes in a manner that perverts Cicero's intention and his authority. This does not happen because our *pregonero* was denied the advantage of a Salamanca education; he is no frustrated, late-blooming latinist. This is one more of Lázaro's studied, deceitful distortions.[18] *Honra* is related to *honos* etymologically, of

[16] In the study mentioned in note 1, I examine Lázaro's misuse of the *deleitar/aprovechar* convention for justifying a text and recognizing the obligations of an author. I reason there that Lázaro's indifference to this commonly respected topos is his author's way of reminding us of its existence, reaffirming it and signaling his disagreement with his narrator. This contradiction amounts to an invitation to his readers to read his fiction with their moral faculties alert and thereby disappoint the narrator's hopes that his witty text will be received primarily as an entertainment and a symbol of solidarity reconciling the laughers and the laugh-master.

[17] Rico ed., p. 6, n. 4; Ricapito ed., p. 93, n. 7.

[18] In an oral society increasingly influenced by writing and printing, casual references such as Lázaro's to Cicero and Pliny (5) are testimony

course; semantically, there is also a kinship between the words, more or less close depending on cases. Both have a range of senses, and their fields overlap. But not here, not in these instances, by which I mean, not in these two contexts. Cicero speaks of honor as an incitement that draws out and socializes (i.e., makes estimable and available for imitation) the best that lies otherwise underesteemed (even disparaged) in the gifted artist. His *honos* is positively connoted; it is associated with excellence, discovery and refinement, and the studious pursuit of that superior standard, "the Greeks."[19] Lázaro's usage is close to an inversion of this; the desire for *honra* is for him, his examples suggest, a low common denominator in human affairs, and the acquisition of honor depends on formal requirements only. Living within the community's previously defined norm, rather than rising above it, is one such requirement. Novelty is not helpful, singular accomplishments are not necessary. What one does matters less—to the soldier, the preacher, the gentleman—than how one is perceived. According to Lázaro's prologue and his narrative as well, honor, deception, pretense, and pretentiousness cohabit in the same semantic field.

The anonymous author and his implied reader are learned; they know their Cicero. A single clue of this sort, prominently displayed at the beginning and worked well into the text, is sufficient early warning from one to the other. You and I, it says, understand Cicero and his claims for honor and art, and rhetoric; know then too that they are twisted by this narrator; he is dishonorable; his misrepresentation reduces to insignificance all that is grand, ele-

---

to the prestige of classical authority but certainly not to the speaker's or writer's first-hand familiarity with his sources. Lázaro, like that other verbal genius, Celestina, before him, has daily intercourse with *amigos y señores* from whom he can easily acquire classical *dicta* to supplement his native proverbial lore. Lázaro's mistranslation of *honos* is noticed and commented on perceptively by Maurice Molho, in *Introducción al pensamiento picaresco* (Salamanca: Anaya, 1972), p. 57.

[19] "Honos alit artes omnesque incenduntur ad studia gloria iacentque ea semper quae apud quosque improbantur" ("Public esteem is the nurse of the arts, and all men are fired to application by fame, whilst those pursuits which meet with general disapproval, always lie neglected"), *Tusculan Disputations*, trans. J. E. King, The Loeb Classical Library (Cambridge: Harvard Univ. Press, 1960), I.4. See also n. 22 for Cicero's preceding comment on the poet's place in society.

vating, discriminating in his source, in Ciceronian rhetoric, in Roman letters and in classical standards; and debasing Cicero, he offends us. The anonymous author in this fashion undercuts his narrator, who has subverted authority. The effect of this irony, however, is not simply to reaffirm the authority of the source. Lázaro and Cicero espouse polar attitudes concerning the functioning of honor as a mediator between a nation and its poets, and while the author rejects the former, he does so without aligning himself with the latter.

If Lázaro's performance is dishonorable and cynical, Cicero's position is untenable in mid-16th-century Spain. The anonymous author is a victim of the truth declared immediately following the phrase Lázaro lifted from Cicero, a worrisome truth that (because it accompanies and is attached to the much-quoted tag) the author may expect his reader to recall to mind: "Honos alit artes, omnesque incenduntur ad studia gloria, *iacentque ea semper, quae apud quosque improbantur.*" Public scorn is ever a stern censor, and the problem recognized here is by no means just a theoretical one for the author and first readers of *Lazarillo*. In their anxious society the notions of what was honorable and what was tolerable had become confused and increasingly circumscribed, and disparagement of intellectual and artistic activities that lay outside the magic circle was institutionalized in forms that could not be more obnoxious for the artist: censorship of texts, suppression of uncongenial expression, and several sorts of intimidation of writers.[20]

Divorcing himself from his narrator's dishonorable posturing, but prevented by circumstances from gaining for himself the public esteem and the nourishment Cicero's formulation promises, what was *Lazarillo's* author to do? How was he to make his claim to being superior as an artist to his boastful creature and deserving of plaudits? His paradoxical solution, recognized some years ago by Stephen Gilman and anticipated before him by Américo Castro: it

[20] The bibliography treating this cluster of problems is now extensive. Particularly recommended for its illumination of the ways exemplary verbalizers came to terms with this situation is Stephen Gilman's *The Spain of Fernando de Rojas* (Princeton: Princeton University Press, 1972), which I have surveyed in *Journal of Hispanic Philology*, 3 (1979-80), 197-238. Also see Gilman's "A Generation of Conversos," *Romance Philology*, 33 (1979-80), 87-101.

is the author's silence that sets him above and distinguishes him ethically from his creature.[21]

Lázaro construes his snippet of Cicero to say that the artist creates in order to gain fame. (He is not different, according to this claim, from anyone else, any soldier, preacher, gentleman: "todo va desta manera" [6].) But our author has created a remarkable work and he has neither claimed nor acknowledged any such reward for his accomplishment. His silence is eloquent contradiction of his narrator's claim. The author knows, and probably expects his reader to recall, that Cicero's analysis is more complex than Lázaro's excerpt suggests. For Lázaro, praise and honor are simply payment for services rendered; Cicero is interested, however, in fluctuating degrees of correspondence between the interests of the artist and those of his community. The latter, in his view, responds by honoring the artist when it esteems his product; the artist gains honor whose work is both finely wrought and socially estimable; and circumstances alter cases. There is in the present case and circumstances no honor-generating coincidental attraction between, on one hand, what the author is capable of saying (because he is a great artist) and deems necessary and urgent to say (because he is an anxious citizen) and, on the other, what the community in general and the powerful in particular will tolerate and reward. He who writes for a fractured community is bound to be judged fractious. If honor depends, as Cicero suggests, on a high degree of coincidence between the individual's and the community's interests, and additionally on the esteem the community feels for the individual's formulation of their coincidental interests, then at the time of its publication there was little honorable about *La vida de Lazarillo de Tormes*. The work was quickly and officially suppressed.

It is clear to us that the author deserved the esteem and has won the honor Cicero had in mind, for his work is distinguished and in time it nourished an art that flourished and called into being a great community of readers. But he was constrained by his immediate situation, and elementary prudence dictated that he keep his own voice stilled. We cannot conclude from this, however, that the difference between our author and his narrator lies in the

[21] Gilman, "The Death of Lazarillo de Tormes," *PMLA*, 81 (1966), at p. 151.

former's prudence and silence. We must remember that for Lázaro to keep silent would be to surrender to those other voices around him and to suffer annihilation; he must write to make us laugh; his voice and his readers' laughing response are all that save him and his *Vida* from "la sepultura del olvido" (5). His is an eccentric and especially threatening variant form of a familiar double bind: he must publish or perish. We, therefore, must acknowledge another paradox: in his case, admittedly an extreme and bizarre one, prudence consists in his making a laughing stock of himself. It is as prudent of him to write, to joke, to publish his story and thereby to invite attention *as a writer,* as it is for his author to keep quiet, to deflect attention from himself, and to publish anonymously. Lázaro writes to stave off attackers; his author, it is reasonable to suppose, keeps silent for the same reason.

By keeping silent, the author demolishes Lázaro's claim that art and other shows of ability are motivated by a universal thirst for praise and fame, and a hunger for advancement and profit. His text is evidence of a compelling counterclaim: some authors are willing to accept great risks, even to prejudice their social standing and hazard humiliation (of the kind *pregoneros* administered in Toledo), in order to express what they must express in the best way possible. His act also suggests that a general truth as significant to us as *honos alit artes* lies imbedded in Cicero's preceding observation concerning the delayed and difficult gestation of Latin poetry: "The lighter the esteem in which poetry was held, the less was the devotion paid to it, and yet such writers as have by virtue of great natural endowments proved themselves poets, have not failed to be a worthy match for the glory of the Greeks."[22] Where novel values are unsupported by the community, they may nevertheless be manifested splendidly, though sporadically, by isolated artists of great ability. Their works then possess art's inexhaustible potential for building a sense of community, if only later, where and when conditions permit, among those who recognize them for what they are. This community, which is not confined by narrow boundaries in time and space, by its very existence honors, belatedly, the artist who convokes it through his art. As the community grows, and with it the esteem, so too, according to Cicero,

---

[22] "Quo minus igitur honoris erat poëtis, eo minora studia fuerunt, nec tamen, si qui magnis ingeniis in eo genere exstiterunt, non satis Graecorum gloriae responderunt" (Cicero, I.3).

the creative consequences. In the case now before us, not for nearly half a century were the efforts of the kind that went into *Lazarillo* pursued—unless, of course, we have in mind the energetic pursuit undertaken by censors, inquisitors, and gossips intent on disrupting such study. But then, amid conditions that inhibited direct questioning, the potential contained in *Lazarillo* began to be recognized by Spain's greatest parabolic visionaries. Our anonymous author, a sort of Unknown Soldier in the war of irony to free us all from arrogant certainty, was then greatly honored, by the study and imitation of his followers—among them Mateo Alemán and Miguel de Cervantes—and by the attention of legions of readers. Retrospectively, and more or less creatively, they and we have come to regard the author of *La vida de Lazarillo de Tormes* in much the same way that Cicero assessed those exceptional early poets: in spite of circumstances, "a worthy match for the glory of the Greeks."

UNIVERSITY OF WASHINGTON

Index of Authors
and Anonymous Works